S0-BFC-223

Lake County Public Library

GRANDPARENTS'

RIGHTS

GRANDPARENTS'
RIGHTS

—

Traci Truly
Attorney at Law

Sphinx Publishing
A Division of Sourcebooks, Inc.
Naperville, IL • Clearwater, FL

LAKE COUNTY PUBLIC LIBRARY

3 3113 01843 8806

Copyright © 1995 and 1999 by Traci Truly
Cover design © 1999 by Sourcebooks, Inc.

All rights reserved. No part of this book may be reproduced in any form or by any electronic or mechanical means including information storage and retrieval systems—except in the case of brief quotations embodied in critical articles or reviews—without permission in writing from its publisher, Sourcebooks, Inc. Purchasers of the book are granted a license to use the forms contained herein for their own personal use. No claim of copyright is made to any official government forms reproduced herein.

Second edition, 1999

Published by: **Sphinx® Publishing, A Division of Sourcebooks, Inc.®**

Naperville Office
P.O. Box 372
Naperville, Illinois 60566
630-961-3900
Fax: 630-961-2168

· Clearwater Office
P.O. Box 25
Clearwater, Florida 33757
727-587-0999
Fax: 727-586-5088

Interior Design and Production: Amy S. Hall/Edward A. Haman, Sourcebooks, Inc.

This publication is designed to provide accurate and authoritative information in regard to the subject matter covered. It is sold with the understanding that the publisher is not engaged in rendering legal, accounting, or other professional service. If legal advice or other expert assistance is required, the services of a competent professional person should be sought.

From a Declaration of Principles Jointly Adopted by a Committee of the American Bar Association and a Committee of Publishers and Associations

Library of Congress Cataloging-in-Publication Data

Truly, Traci.
    Grandparent's rights / Traci Truly. -- 2nd ed.
        p.   cm.
    Includes index.
    ISBN 1-57248-082-3 (pbk.)
    1. Custody of children--United States--Popular works.
  2. Visitation rights (Domestic relations)--United States--Popular works. 3. Grandparents--Legal status, laws, etc.--United States--Popular works. I. Title.
    KF547.Z9T78   1999
346.7301'73--dc21

98-55580
CIP

Printed and bound in the United States of America.

Paperback — 10 9 8 7 6 5 4 3 2 1

CONTENTS

USING SELF-HELP LAW BOOKS

Whenever you shop for a product or service, you encounter various levels of quality and price. In deciding what product or service to buy, you make a cost/value analysis on the basis of your willingness to pay and the quality you desire.

When buying a car, you decide whether you want transportation, comfort, status, or sex appeal. Accordingly, you decide among such choices as a Neon, a Lincoln, a Rolls Royce, or a Porsche. Before making a decision, you usually weigh the merits of each option against the cost.

When you get a headache, you can take a pain reliever (such as aspirin) or visit a medical specialist for a neurological examination. Given this choice, most people, of course, take a pain reliever, since it costs only pennies; whereas a medical examination costs hundreds of dollars and takes a lot of time. This is usually a logical choice because rarely is anything more than a pain reliever needed for a headache. But in some cases, a headache may indicate a brain tumor, and failing to see a specialist right away can result in complications. Should everyone with a headache go to a specialist? Of course not, but people treating their own illnesses must realize that they are betting on the basis of their cost/value analysis of the situation, they are taking the most logical option.

The same cost/value analysis must be made in deciding to do one's own legal work. Many legal situations are very straight forward, requiring a simple form and no complicated analysis. Anyone with a little intelligence and a book of instructions can handle the matter without outside help.

But there is always the chance that complications are involved that only an attorney would notice. To simplify the law into a book like this, several legal cases often must be condensed into a single sentence or paragraph. Otherwise, the book would be several hundred pages long and too complicated for most people. However, this simplification necessarily leaves out many details and nuances that would apply to special or unusual situations. Also, there are many ways to interpret most legal questions. Your case may come before a judge who disagrees with the analysis of our authors.

Therefore, in deciding to use a self-help law book and to do your own legal work, you must realize that you are making a cost/value analysis and deciding that the chance your case will not turn out to your satisfaction is outweighed by the money you will save in doing it yourself. Most people handling their own simple legal matters never have a problem, but occasionally people find that it ended up costing them more to have an attorney straighten out the situation than it would have if they had hired an attorney in the beginning. Keep this in mind while handling your case, and be sure to consult an attorney if you feel you might need further guidance.

INTRODUCTION

The purpose of this book is to help you (a grandparent) secure visitation with, or obtain custody of, your grandchildren without hiring a lawyer. Even if you do decide to hire a lawyer, this book will help you to work with your lawyer more efficiently and effectively.

This is not a law school course, but a practical guide to get you through "The System" as comfortably as possible. Legal jargon has been nearly eliminated. The emphasis is on practical information in plain English. For ease of understanding, certain terms and language will be used in order to avoid confusion when talking about the grandparents, the parents, and the grandchildren. This book is written in language which assumes that you (the reader) are a grandparent, therefore, the words "you" and "grandparent" will be used interchangeably. The word "parent" refers to the parent of your grandchild. The word "grandchild" will be used instead of the word "child," so that there is no confusion about whether it is your grandchild or your son or daughter who is being discussed. Occasionally, it will be necessary to refer to "your son or daughter" to distinguish between the parent to whom you are related and the other parent. Finally, the words "parent" and "parents," and "grandchild" and "grandchildren" are used interchangeably.

One difficulty in writing a book of this type is that court procedures and laws are different in every state and sometimes in various courts in the same state. While general forms are provided in appendix C of this book, you will need to do some research to determine exactly what forms are required for your state and county. More will be discussed about this later in this book.

Be sure to read the entire book before you begin preparing any of the forms in this book. You may want to make several copies of the forms in this book and save the originals in order to make more copies if you need them.

Overview of Grandparents' Rights

1

The relationship between grandparents and their grandchildren has become increasingly complex and less traditional over the past ten to twenty years. More and more, grandparents find themselves looking to the courts to set the parameters of their time with their grandchildren. The rising divorce rate, soaring single parenthood, increased drug use among the adult population, and a troubled economy have all played a part in these changes as they have altered the entire American family structure.

For various reasons, a significant number of grandparents have assumed full-time responsibility for rearing their grandchildren. An even greater number have sought the assistance of the courts to get regular visitation with their grandchildren. As a result, the various state legislatures have been forced to set standards for grandparent visitation and for custody to nonparents.

The purpose of this book is to examine the laws of the various states regarding grandparent visitation and custody. Additionally, a review will be made of different family and fact situations that can affect your decision to file for custody or visitation. You will also learn about court proceedings involved in custody and visitation cases.

If you decide to go to court to seek custody of, or visitation with, your grandchildren, one of the decisions you will have to make is whether or not to hire an attorney. Chapter 6 will address the various factors involved in that decision as well as the pluses and minuses of representing yourself in court. You will also receive an overview of the types of evidence you will need in order to prepare a custody or visitation case.

Obviously, the laws relating to grandparent visitation and custody vary from state to state. In the back of this book you will find appendix A, which contains summaries of the laws of each state. Before you file on your own, you will need to study the law of your state to be sure you meet the qualifications to file and to be sure you know how to file.

KINDS OF RIGHTS AVAILABLE

There are two basic types of rights available to grandparents in relation to their grandchildren: custody and visitation. *Custody* refers to the legal rights and obligations that go along with assuming the role of full-time parent to your grandchildren. Deciding to file for custody of your grandchildren involves making a big commitment, especially if the children's parents fight your attempt to obtain custody. In that event, you should review your situation very carefully before you file.

The second right is that of *visitation*. Simply, this involves the court setting a schedule for you to spend time with your grandchildren. Once again, the laws vary from state to state and you will need to study appendix A before you file. The fact that you are not getting to see your grandchildren may not, by itself, be enough to qualify you for court-ordered visitation.

LEGAL RESEARCH

Once you have reviewed this book and studied your state's listing in appendix A carefully, you will need to consult your nearest law library or public library with a legal section. If your public library does not have a legal section, or if it does not contain the information you need, you may be able to find a law library in or near your county courthouse. If you live near a law school, you will also find a library there. The librarian will be able to direct you to the proper books, but cannot tell you what forms to use or how to fill them out because they are not allowed to give legal advice. In the legal section, you will find several types of books.

STATUTES OR CODES

One set of books that you will need to use is the set of statutes or codes. These are the books in which the laws passed by the state legislature are found. You will find references to these books in the state law section in appendix A. You will notice that many of the state statutes have the words *revised* or *annotated* in the title. (For example: *Vernon's Texas Codes Annotated* and the *Hawaii Revised Statutes*.) *Annotated* just means that the statutes also contain a listing of some court cases that have been decided under a particular section of the statute and a summary of the court decision immediately following the text of the statute section itself. *Revised* means the books have been updated with changes in the laws. The *Vernon's* in the Texas statute example above refers to the publisher. Many state statutes contain the name of the publisher in the book title.

Every time your state legislature meets, it is possible that some change to the law that governs your case will be made. It is important that you use the most current version of the law. Therefore, when you look in these books, be sure you check for the most current supplements. These may be found attached to the main volume or in a soft cover book kept near the main volume.

PRACTICE MANUALS

You will also find practice manuals which contain forms and practical pointers for handling different kinds of cases. If there is a conflict between the forms contained in this book and the forms you find in a practice manual for your state, you should use the form from the practice manual that is tailored specifically for your state.

COURT RULES   These books contain the procedural rules for your state. For example, the rules about how to notify people of court filings and hearing dates will be found here.

REPORTERS   Another set of books that will be helpful to you is the *reporter*. These books contain the written opinions of courts, usually appellate courts, as to how and why each case was decided the way it was. The cases for your state will be found in the reporter for your region. The following is a list of reporters and the states they cover:

ABBREVIATION	FULL NAME OF REPORTER	STATES COVERED
A. and A.2d	Atlantic Reporter	Connecticut, Delaware, District of Columbia, Maine, Maryland, New Hampshire, New Jersey, Pennsylvania, Rhode Island, Vermont
Cal. Rptr. and Cal. Rptr.2d	California Reporter	California
N.E. and N.E.2d	Northeastern Reporter	Illinois, Indiana, Massachusetts, New York, Ohio; also New York Court of Appeals
N.Y.S.	New York Supplement	New York
N.W. and N.W.2d	Northwestern Reporter	Iowa, Michigan, Minnesota, Nebraska, North Dakota, South Dakota, Wisconsin
P. and P.2d	Pacific Reporter	Alaska, Arizona, California Supreme Court since 1960, Colorado, Hawaii, Idaho, Kansas, Montana, Nevada, New Mexico, Oklahoma, Oregon, Utah, Washington, Wyoming
S.E. and S.E.2d	Southeastern Reporter	Georgia, North Carolina, South Carolina, Virginia, West Virginia
So. and So.2d	Southern Reporter	Alabama, Florida, Louisiana, Mississippi
S.W. and S.W.2d	Southwestern Reporter	Arkansas, Kentucky, Missouri, Tennessee, Texas

A case will be cited as follows: *Jones v. Jones*, 750 S.W.2d 859 (Tex. 1985). You would find this case by looking in volume 750 of the *Southwestern Reporter 2nd Series* and turning to page 859. The "(Tex. 1985)" means that the Texas Supreme Court decided the case in 1985. Sometimes you will see a fairly recent case cited something like: "*Smith v. Smith*, No. 2920-39 (Cal. 1999)." This is a case that is too recent to have made its way to the reporter; and the citation refers to the case number used by the particular appellate court.

DIGESTS

One way to locate particular cases that apply to your situation is by looking at the annotations following the statute itself; another source is the *digest*. There will be a digest for your state and it will contain brief summaries of cases and tell you where to find the full text of the opinion. The cases are grouped together in this set of books according to subject matter. The digest will contain an index to help you find the right subject heading.

LEGAL ENCYCLOPEDIAS

A *legal encyclopedia* can also be good sources of information. *American Jurisprudence* and *Corpus Juris Secundum* are two that are national in scope, but your state may have its own. (*Texas Jurisprudence* is an example of a state legal encyclopedia.) Once again, the material will be grouped by subject matter. In this book, you will find a summary of the laws on the particular subject and a few cases listed.

You should check with the law librarian to see what is available for your state. The law is constantly changing, and you need to check to see if the courts have changed the interpretation of the statute as it is written or if the state legislature has amended the statute itself. Once you have done these things, you will be better prepared to confront the legal system, either on your own or with the assistance of a lawyer.

SUMMARY OF CUSTODY LAWS

All fifty states have passed some form of grandparent visitation (the District of Columbia has not, however) and, of course, all have laws governing child custody. In terms of custody, all states have adopted a form of a law called the *Uniform Child Custody Jurisdiction Act* (UCCJA). This law is basically designed to provide a method for resolving disputes between courts when more than one state is involved. In today's mobile society, it is not unusual for parents to have been married in one state, lived in several others, separated, and moved to two more states. UCCJA sets out the guidelines for determining which state should have the primary right to rule on child custody issues in a particular case. If you are in a situation where more than one state is involved, you will need to study this law and comply with its provisions. There are, however, additional laws in each state governing child custody.

In each case, you will need to review the laws of the state in which the court that will decide the custody case is located. A number of states have fairly specific statutes setting out the factors to be considered in deciding custody, and you will need to tailor your evidence to these factors. Other states will give you very little guidance in the statute. For example, it may only say that the "best interest of the child" is the controlling factor. If your custody case is filed in one of these states, you will need to read some of the court decisions that have interpreted the custody statute so that you know what will and will not be helpful to you in the way of evidence. Even if your state has a fairly specific statute, you would be well advised to read some of the cases as suggested above. Actually, those states which do give specific factors are really just trying to explain and define the general concept of "best interest of the child."

SUMMARY OF VISITATION LAWS

In addition to custody, grandparent visitation is governed by statute and by case law interpreting the statute. Each state has slightly different requirements governing the eligibility for visitation. In some states, the only thing you need to show the court is that you have had a substantial past relationship with the child, or that the visitation is in the child's best interest. Other states require that some other proceeding relating to custody or support of the child be pending or have taken place before a grandparent is entitled to visitation. Many states permit visitation when one of the child's parents is deceased. Some states are more restrictive about grandparent visitation while others are quite liberal. In three states, Florida, Tennessee and Washington, courts have recently ruled that the state grandparent visitation statute is unconstitutional. Each of these areas will be discussed in greater detail in the following chapters.

SHOULD YOU FILE FOR VISITATION? 2

If you are contemplating seeking the court's assistance in getting visitation, it is probably because you are having difficulty with one or more of the parents and are not seeing your grandchildren regularly. Or perhaps there are problems in your grandchildren's home environment. You most likely tried to reach some kind of agreement with the parents but were not successful; otherwise you would probably not be reading this book. The assumption here is that the parents are unwilling to allow you visitation. However, you should still be willing to settle the issue by agreement even after you file your lawsuit for visitation.

RECENT DEVELOPMENTS

This chapter, as well as chapter 3, are written based upon the grandparent visitation laws that are "on the books" in the various states. You need to be aware that these laws are always subject to change, either by the state legislature or by court decisions. Recent state supreme court cases in Florida, Tennessee, and Washington have declared those states' grandparent visitation laws unconstitutional. As all three of these state court decisions were decided on the same basis, it is possible that this is the beginning of a trend that will extend to other states. Even if you don't live in one of these states, it will be helpful for you to understand the reasoning of these courts as this question may be brought up in your case by the parents or their attorney. Therefore, we will briefly examine these cases.

In the Tennessee case [*Hawk v. Hawk*, 855 S.W.2d 573 (Tenn. 1993)], the Tennessee Supreme Court said that the United States Constitution, through its guarantee of privacy, prohibits the government from unreasonably interfering with a parent's right to raise his or children as the parent sees fit. The court determined that the Tennessee grandparent visitation statute was such an unreasonable interference with the rights of parents. The statute was changed after this court decision, but the new statute may not have solved the constitutional problem.

In the first of two Florida Supreme Court cases, *Beagle v. Beagle*, 678 So.2d 1271 (Fla. 1996), grandparents sought visitation where the child's parents were still living together. The Court said that the Florida grandparent visitation statute violated the parents' right to privacy under the Florida Constitution.

In *Von Eiff v. Azicri*, No. 91,647 (Fla. 1998), visitation was sought by grandparents whose daughter had died. The Florida Supreme Court again found the visitation statute to violate the surviving parent's right to privacy in raising his child, saying:

> Neither the legislature nor the courts may properly intervene in parental decisionmaking absent significant harm to the child threatened by or resulting from those decisions....[O]therwise fit parents...who have neither abused, neglected, or abandoned their child, have a reasonable expectation that the state will not interfere with their decision to exclude or limit the grandparents' visitation with their child.

The Washington case [*In re the Custody of Sara Skyanne Smith*, No. 65605-3 (Wash. 1998)], the court used the same reasoning as the Florida case, that forcing grandparent visitation interferes with parents' rights to raise their children, and would only be justified if the child is threatened with harm. However, even if there is abuse or neglect, it would not seem that visitation would alleviate the problem. In such a case, you would probably be seeking custody.

If you live in Florida, Tennessee, or Washington, or if you find that your state's courts have followed the lead of these three, you should seek the advice of an attorney before filing a petition for visitation.

REASONS TO FILE

A variety of situations may exist that will indicate whether an action for grandparent visitation may be appropriate. For example, if the parents are engaged in a bitter divorce and custody battle and you have always been close to your grandchildren, court ordered visitation may help give the grandchildren some continuity and stability. This may particularly be the case when you, as grandparents, are the parents of the non-custodial parent. In those instances, the custodial parent may be unwilling to permit the soon-to-be-former-in-laws to visit the grandchildren. As the parents of the non-custodial parent, you may not want to infringe on your son's or daughter's limited time with his or her children. It may be necessary, therefore, to seek the court's assistance in carving some additional time from the custodial parent's time. Other situations that are good candidates for court-ordered visitation are where your child is the non-custodial parent and lives a great distance from you, or when you do not have a particularly good relationship with your child and do not see your grandchildren when they are in your child's possession.

If one or both of the parents have died, you may consider filing in order to continue a regular relationship with the grandchild. This is especially true if your child is the parent who is deceased. The remaining parent may not emphasize keeping up family contact with the deceased parent's relatives. Here, court-ordered visitation is generally available.

However, one word of warning: any time your grandchild is adopted by someone, you may lose all rights in relation to that child. This is because the rights of the biological parents are terminated in an adoption proceeding. A parent whose rights have been terminated is legally a stranger to the child, and so are the grandparents. Legally, the child is no longer your grandchild. Nonetheless, the majority of states have an exception to the termination of grandparent visitation rights if the adoption is by a stepparent or other relative. Conversely, if your son or daughter adopts a child, you will qualify for grandparent rights to that grandchild if you meet the requirements in your state.

Another reason you might consider filing for visitation is if the non-custodial parent does not, or cannot, exercise visitation periods. If you qualify under the statute, the court is likely to find that the visits are in your grandchild's best interest because they serve to strengthen your grandchild's sense of family.

If the parents are unstable, either emotionally or financially, and you otherwise qualify for visitation in your state, visitation may be important not only for your grandchild's security, but also for allowing you an informal way of monitoring your grandchild's situation to see if more serious action needs to be taken.

If you are seeing your grandchildren but there is frequent conflict over scheduling, having the court set ground rules may remove a source of conflict. This will also assure that you get at least some regular contact with your grandchild, and you avoid being at the mercy of one or both parents regarding your time with your grandchildren. Certainly, you may expect opposition from your own son or daughter as well as the other parent.

In a situation where your relationship with both parents is bad, court intervention may be your only hope of maintaining a relationship with your grandchildren. Although the fact that you have a poor relationship with the parents may be used by the parents in an attempt to block the visitation you have requested, courts generally realize that the grandparent statutes were passed in the first place to accommodate families with fractured relationships. Most judges will expect some difficulties in the relationship between the parents and grandparents and will not be unduly alarmed if the parents oppose you.

REASONS NOT TO FILE

The reasons behind that opposition, however, may be very costly to your bid for grandparent visitation. If there are allegations substantiated by evidence that you have been abusive, either physically, emotionally, or sexually, to any child, the court can certainly find that visitation with you is not in the best interest of your grandchildren and deny your request. In some states, a conviction for child abuse automatically excludes you from obtaining visitation. Even in states where such a conviction is not a statutory exclusion, you should recognize the difficulty of convincing the court that visitation with you is in your grandchild's best interest.

One of the pitfalls of seeking court-ordered visitation is that you may do permanent damage to your relationship with your son or daughter. Any unresolved emotional issues between you and your son or daughter will likely flare up if you file a lawsuit against your son or daughter demanding visitation with your grandchildren. If you are in this sort of situation, you must weigh the possible problems caused with your own son or daughter against the need for court intervention in order for you to see your grandchildren. In a situation where the relationship between the parents and grandparents is poor, it is important for all parties to remember that the grandchild loves all of you, benefits from a close relationship with all of you, and does not belong in the middle of a bitter court battle between his parents and grandparents. None of you should disparage the other to your grandchild. It is vital for the grandparents to determine whether the benefit to the grandchild of court-ordered visitation outweighs any problems this will cause at home for your grandchild with parents who resent your intervention.

There are also cost factors, both in terms of time and money, even if you elect to represent yourself. If you are getting some access now, you may not be able to improve your situation enough to offset the financial and emotional costs of going to court. You must also give consideration to the age of your grandchildren. Courts may be reluctant to send infants

17

off for visitation periods in order to avoid trauma to the child. Courts are also hesitant to order unwilling, uninterested teens to go for visitation with a grandparent and will likely encourage the teen, the parents, and the grandparents to resolve the issues themselves without the help of the court.

Some courts are more generous than others in the amount of access they typically give to grandparents. You may get as little as a few hours every two or three months or as much as a weekend every month. You should not realistically expect to approach the level of the every other weekend schedule normally available to the non-custodial parent. Of course, the circumstances of your particular case may warrant an exception to any general rules or policies. The amount of grandparent access is left strictly to the discretion of the judge. You may want to make inquiries or consult an attorney to get an idea of what policies the judge who will hear your case has for grandparent visitation.

REQUIREMENTS AND QUALIFICATIONS

PARENTS
PRESENTLY
MARRIED

The requirements and qualifications for visitation are dependent in many states on the status of the parents' relationship. In the majority of states, you will not be entitled to visitation if your grandchild's parents are still married to each other and living together. Only Connecticut, Delaware, Idaho, Kentucky, Maine, Montana, New York, North Dakota, Oklahoma, Tennessee, and Wisconsin have statutes providing for visitation while the parents are still together, with the only requirement in most of these being that the visitation be in the grandchild's best interest. Some of these add requirements, such as that the grandparent has established a substantial relationship with their grandchild (Idaho and Maine); that some special condition exists which necessitates consideration of grandparent visitation (New York); that the visitation not interfere with the parent-child relationship (North Dakota); or that a relationship exists between the grandparent and grandchild that is similar to the parent-child relationship (Wisconsin).

In some states, grandparents may be entitled to visitation while the parents are still married if certain other conditions are present. In three states (Arkansas, Colorado, and Iowa), grandparents may petition for visitation if the grandchild is in the custody of someone other than the parents, regardless of the status of the parents' relationship. If one of the parents is absent, Arizona, California, and Florida statutes provide for grandparent visitation. If the grandparents have been denied visitation for a specified period of time, several states provide for visitation even if the parents remain together. These states are Alabama, Missouri, New Mexico, Pennsylvania, Rhode Island, West Virginia, and Wyoming. Minnesota allows for visitation if the grandchild has previously resided with the grandparents. Illinois allows visitation if one of the parents joins the grandparents in the request. In South Carolina, the grandparent must show exceptional circumstances to get visitation. Texas also has provisions for grandparent visitation under certain conditions while the parents remain married; for example, if one parent is in jail or if the grandchild has been abused or neglected. Many of the states listed above allow for visitation under more than one of the type of situation described above. For a complete list of situations giving rise to visitation, you will need to refer to the listing for your state in appendix A and to the statutes for your particular state.

PENDING DIVORCE

In most states, the filing of a petition for divorce, dissolution of marriage, or for legal separation triggers eligibility to file for grandparent visitation. In some states, it is sufficient that some sort of proceeding for custody or separate maintenance be filed to authorize a request for grandparent visitation, even if there is not a request to dissolve the marriage before the court. In Illinois, Massachusetts, Mississippi, and New Jersey, physical separation as opposed to legal separation is a ground for grandparent visitation.

PARENTS ALREADY DIVORCED

Arizona requires that the parents' marriage have been dissolved for at least three months before grandparent visitation is permitted. Florida, Indiana, and Maryland provide for visitation after dissolution of the marriage.

19

DECEASED
PARENT

All states that have specific requirements relating to the condition of the parents' marriage in order to qualify for grandparent visitation treat the death of a parent as a condition giving rise to visitation. The laws vary as to which grandparents qualify to apply for visitation when a parent dies. Some states permit visitation for either set of grandparents in the case of the death of a parent. Other states limit the visitation to the parents of the deceased parent of the child. As always, you will need to check the statute for your state to see which version applies to you and to determine whether or not there are any additional requirements that apply in this situation; for example, Wyoming allows visitation in this situation only if the grandparent's child has died and the person having custody of the grandchild has refused visitation.

CHILDREN
BORN OUT OF
WEDLOCK

Another condition which may enable grandparents to seek visitation is when the child has been born out of wedlock. Many states have specific provisions for this situation. As a general rule, mothers of children born out of wedlock have full parental rights to that child; fathers, however, have no parental rights to the child until some action is taken under the paternity or parentage laws to declare them the legal father. Since most states require that the father be declared the child's legal father (using the procedures set out in the paternity or parentage laws) for grandparent visitation to be awarded, paternal grandparents will need to determine the status of their son's legal relationship to the child in order to know whether they are eligible for grandparent visitation.

NATIVE
AMERICAN
CHILDREN

If your grandchild is a Native American, you will need to review a specific Federal law: the Indian Child Welfare Act. This law may govern some or all of your case, and may even override the law of your particular state.

FILING FOR VISITATION 3

Now that you have made the decision to file in court for visitation, the next step is to prepare your paperwork for filing. How and what to file depends on the status of any legal proceedings between the parents, the contents of the specific state statute for grandparent visitation, and the provisions of the state procedural rules. In addition to the information contained in this book, you will need to refer to the procedural rules for your state.

Generally, the petition should contain the names of the grandparents seeking visitation; the names and addresses and dates of birth of the grandchildren with whom visitation is sought; the names and addresses of the parents and any other individuals or entities with court-ordered relationships with the children; the grounds from the statute that authorizes your visitation (see appendix A); and a request that the court order the visitation. You will find additional information about how to complete the forms and file them in chapter 7. Massachusetts provides a standard complaint form in the grandparent visitation statute. For illustration purposes, refer to form B in appendix B, which is the Massachusetts complaint form that has been filled in using the following facts: John Doe and his wife, Jane, are the parents of Robert Doe, who was married to Wanda Smith in 1980. Robert and Wanda have two children, Sam Doe and Sara Doe. Sam is thirteen and Sara is six. In 1992, Robert and Wanda were divorced in Massachusetts. Wanda got custody of the children and Robert was awarded visitation. In their Judgment of Divorce, no mention was made of the grandparents. John and Jane have decided to go to court and file for visitation. The document they would file with the court in order to begin the proceedings is set out as form B in appendix B. With some modifications, this form should be sufficient in most states.

Some states, however, have additional requirements. Massachusetts also requires that a care and custody affidavit be included. Some type of affidavit is also required in Colorado, Florida, Maine, and Michigan. New York specifically requires that the action be brought by a *special proceeding* or by *writ of habeas corpus*. (These are names of legal proceedings and documents. You will need to refer to additional sources for New York to determine the requirements for these proceedings.)

MEDIATION

Missouri has created an additional procedure for resolution of grandparent disputes that does not require the filing of a formal complaint. Section 452.403 of Vernon's Annotated Missouri Statutes permits a grandparent who has been denied visitation to make a written request for mediation. In that event, the court can order all parties with custody and visitation rights to attend a session with a neutral mediator appointed by the court. This mediator will attempt to help the parties reach an agreement about visitation rights for the grandparents. The mediator does not have the power to order the parents to permit visitation; he or she can only facilitate a voluntary agreement. One warning: the statute requires the grandparents to bear all of the costs of the mediation. Form 11 in appendix C is the Missouri form to request mediation. Many other states will have provisions that allow for mediation between the parties at some point during the litigation. Information regarding mediation may be found in the grandparent visitation statutes in some states, in the general domestic relations code in other states, in the state procedural rules, or in the statutes relating to "Alternative Dispute Resolution."

PENDING CASE

If you are seeking grandparent visitation as a part of a divorce or other legal proceeding between the parents, your request should be in the form of an intervention in the parent's case. A sample Texas intervention using the Doe family from the Massachusetts complaint (but changing the facts so that the grandparents are making their request for visitation as a part of the parent's divorce) is included in appendix B as form C. A sample Texas order for grandparent visitation based on the post-divorce complaint, as opposed to the intervention in the pending divorce, is included in appendix B as form H.

ADOPTIONS

Timing can be very important, particularly when adoption is involved. If your son or daughter is giving up his or her parental rights, you may lose your grandparent rights if you do not file your petition before your child's parental rights are terminated. This may be true even if the law in your state says that adoption does not automatically terminate your rights as grandparents.

GREAT-GRANDPARENTS

If you are great-grandparents, you will need to check the laws of your state carefully. Some states specifically include great-grandparents in their visitation laws, while other states exclude great-grandparents. There are also states whose statutes do not address this issue at all.

PREPARING YOUR PETITION

LEGAL FORMS

In all cases, you begin legal proceedings by filing some sort of initial paper. It will usually be called a *complaint* or a *petition*. These documents vary depending on the type of case and type of proceeding. Everything that you file with the court should be typed and double spaced. Some states require that documents be filed on legal sized paper, some states require letter size. You can find out what the requirements for your state are by asking the court clerk. All documents have a heading, called the *case style*. Case styles vary from state to state. To find out what form is appropriate for your state, ask the clerk to let you see a pending case file, or look in a form book in your law library. Generally, the style will contain the name of the state and county and the court designation (*13th District Court*, for example), as well as the names of the parties.

There will also be a docket number assigned to your case. If you are intervening in a pending divorce case, the docket number for your pleadings will be the docket number assigned to the divorce case. If you are filing a new lawsuit, leave this line blank on your first pleading. The clerk will assign you a number when you file the pleading. Use that number for all future filings in that case.

Just before the body of your pleading should be the title of the document. Refer to the forms included in appendix B. They have titles like *Petition in Intervention* and *Complaint for Grandparent Visitation.* All your documents should have titles like this, and the title will vary depending on what you are filing. Visit your law library, or look at a case at the court clerk's office, to find out what title to use. Some states use the word *complaint*; whereas others use the word *petition*. Similarly, some states use the words *plaintiff* and *defendant*; whereas others use *petitioner* and *respondent*. Some may even use *petitioner* and *defendant*.

A typical case style might be as follows:

```
      IN THE FAMILY COURT OF THE STATE OF WASHINGTON,
              IN AND FOR THE COUNTY OF KING

JOHN DOE and JANE DOE,

              Plaintiffs,

VS.                            CASE NO.   99-2394-A

ROBERT DOE and WANDA DOE,

              Defendants.

          COMPLAINT FOR GRANDPARENT VISITATION
```

The same basic information will be included in the case style for all states, although different states will vary the order or location on the page of the information. If you look at forms 2, 3, and 4 in appendix C, you will see examples of the variations for Florida, Massachusetts, and Texas. Except for the forms for these three states, you will find a blank area at the top of each form which covers approximately the top one-third of the page. This should give you enough room to type in the proper case style for your state and county.

At the end of your pleadings, you should close with a paragraph telling the judge what it is you want him or her to do. For example, look at paragraph 4 of the Complaint for Grandparent Visitation found in appendix B as form A. Additionally, you should always sign your documents and then type in your name, address, and phone number. Some states have fill-in-the-blank forms or "check off" forms. Before you begin preparing this paperwork, check with the court clerk to see if they have forms available. If they do, use the forms from the clerk.

The forms contained in appendices B and C of this book are either generic or geared to a specific state. This is because the forms vary from state to state. You may use the forms in this book as a guide, but you should be sure you have adapted the form to fit your particular state.

COMPLAINT/
PETITION FOR
GRANDPARENT
VISITATION
(FORM 1)

Form 1 is a general complaint or petition form for use in seeking visitation in all states except Florida, Massachusetts, and Texas (these states have their own forms which are discussed in the following subsections of this chapter. However, after researching the requirements for your state, you may find you need to modify this form. (For an example of this form completed, see form A in appendix B.) *Warning:* If you live in Tennessee or Washington, be sure to read "Recent Developments" on page 13 about recent Tennessee and Washington Supreme Court decisions before preparing this form or taking any other action to seek a court order for visitation. To complete:

1. Complete the case style portion of the form according to the information in the previous section of this chapter. Follow the language and format commonly used in your state and county.

2. In the first (unnumbered) paragraph, fill in the names of the grandparents seeking visitation on the first line. The second line (after the phrase *hereinafter called the...*) is for your designation as a party; your state will likely use either *Plaintiff, Petitioner* or *Movant.* In the third line, type in the word *Complaint*, or *Petition*, or whatever word or phrase you used as a title. In the line after the word *against*, type in the name or names of the parents (the

same person or persons listed as defendants or respondents in the case style). The last line is for the parents' designation, which will be either *Defendant* or *Respondent*.

3. Paragraph #1 is to identify the relationship of all of the parties. On the first line, type in your designation as a party (*Plaintiff, Petitioner,* or *Movant*). On the second line, type in either *maternal grandparents* or *paternal grandparents,* whichever applies to you. Type your address on the third line. The next two lines are for the parents' designation as parties (*Defendants* or *Respondents*), and their address. If they are living apart, list both addresses (see form A in appendix B for an example of this). In the last two lines, type in the names of the children (your state may also require their ages or birth dates to be listed; if you aren't sure, you may want to include them just to be safe), and their current address.

4. Paragraph #2 is for you to state the legal *grounds* for why you are entitled to visitation. The first blank in the grounds section should contain either your name or your party designation (*Plaintiff, Petitioner,* or *Movant*). The second blank is where you enter the items from your state statute under which you qualify for visitation. Be sure to read the listing for your state in appendix A, and consult your state's statutes before filling in this space. It is a good idea to use the language of your state's grandparent visitation statute as closely as possible. For example, the listing for Alabama in appendix A gives three grounds for a grandparent filing for visitation: 1) there is a divorce pending; 2) one parent is deceased and the surviving parent denies reasonable visitation; and 3) the grandparent has been denied visitation for a period exceeding 90 days. If you fall into the third category, you would type in something like: "The Plaintiffs have been unreasonably denied visitation with the children for a period exceeding 90 days."

5. Paragraph #3 is for you to tell the court if there is any other case pending which relate to visitation or custody. In the blank, type

in your designation as *Plaintiff, Petitioner* or *Movant*. If there are no other cases, type in the word *none* in the space after this paragraph. If there is another case, type in the case style from that other case (name of the court, parties' names, and case number).

6.   Paragraph #4 is for you to tell the judge what you are asking him or her to do. The first blank in the relief section is for your designation as *Plaintiff, Petitioner* or *Movant*. In the second blank, state the specific visitation schedule you want. See forms A and C in appendix B for an example of how this might be completed.

7.   Fill in the date, sign your name, and fill in the name, address, and telephone number information on the appropriate lines.

PETITION/
REQUEST FOR
VISITATION BY
GRANDPARENT
(FORM 2)

Form 2 is the form designed for use in filing for grandparent visitation in Florida. **Warning:** Before preparing this form, and before doing anything about seeking a visitation order in Florida, be sure to read "Recent Developments" on page 13 about recent Florida Supreme Court decisions. To complete:

1.   Type in the number of the judicial circuit and the county where the court is located in the first two lines of the case style. This should be the court for the county where your grandchild lives.

2.   Fill in your name (and your spouse's if you are both filing) on the lines above the word *Grandparent(s)*, and the names of your grandchild's parents on the lines above the word *Respondent(s)*.

3.   Type in your name (and your spouse's if you are both filing) on the line in the first, unnumbered paragraph.

4.   In paragraph 3, fill in the name, birth date, age, and sex of each grandchild with whom you seek visitation.

5.   In paragrah 4, check the appropriate boxes to fit your situation.

6.   In paragraph 5, check the lines before any items that apply to your case. If you check *a* or *c*, you will need to check the appropriate box for *mother* or *father*. The items in paragraph 5 are the

statutory grounds for a grandparent obtaining visitation in Florida. If none of these situations apply, your petition will be dismissed.

7. In paragraph 6, describe the visitation you would like. For example: "Unsupervised visitation, in our home, on the third Saturday of each month, from 9:00 a.m. to 6:00 p.m."

8. In paragraph 7, type in a brief explanation of why you believe the visitation will be in the best interest of your grandchild. For example: "The grandchild has developed an emotional attachment and relationship with the grandparents, and such visitations will be the only opportunity for the child to maintain this relationship and to see his aunts, uncles, and cousins."

9. You (and your spouse if filing together) need to sign before a notary public on the appropriate signature line, and type in your name, address, and phone information on the lines below the signature line. One of you will need to do this on the second page of the form, and the other on the third page.

10. Complete form 6, the Uniform Child Custody Jurisdiction Act Affidavit, and file both forms with the circuit court clerk. These will need to be served on the parents by the sheriff or other approved process server.

COMPLAINT FOR GRANDPARENT VISITATION (FORM 3)

Form 3 is the form you will use if you are filing in Massachusetts. (See the example of this, as form B in appendix B.) To complete:

1. The first two blanks you see (for the *Division* and *Docket No.*) should be left blank. If a division needs to be filled in, you can get this information from the clerk and fill in the blank. The docket number should be left blank; the clerk will assign your case a number when you file the complaint.

2. The blank above the word *Plaintiffs* is where you put in the names of the grandparents seeking visitation.

3. The blank line above the word *Defendants* is for the names of the parents.

4. In #1 on the form, you should put the full names and dates of birth of each of the grandchildren. The address of the grandchildren goes in the second blank.

5. The first blank in #2 on the form is to identify which grandparents, paternal or maternal, are seeking visitation. Your address goes in the second blank.

6. #3 contains blanks for the names and addresses of the parents.

7. #4 is the section in which you identify for the court the grounds under which you are eligible for visitation. Item *a* should be self-explanatory—just fill in the date of the parents' divorce if you are using the parents' divorce to qualify. Items *b* and *c* refer to children born out of wedlock. Use *b* if there was a contested court proceeding that determined the child's father. Item *c* is for use when the parents have followed the procedure whereby they both acknowledged paternity. Item *d* should be checked if you are relying on the separation of the parents as your visitation ground. Note that the parents must have been to court to obtain temporary orders before you can get visitation. Check *e* if one of the parents is dead, and *f* if both parents have died.

8. When you have completed the form, sign and date it, and fill in the name, address, and telephone number information on the appropriate lines.

ORIGINAL PETITION FOR GRANDPARENT VISITATION (FORM 4)

Form 4 is for use in Texas if there is no divorce or other lawsuit pending involving custody or visitation. This form is self-explanatory as to what information needs to be filled in on each line. (For an example of this form completed, see form D in appendix B.) To complete:

1. In the case style section, leave the case number line blank—the clerk will assign the number. The grandchildren's names go in the space just below the words, *In the interest of.*

2. Your names go in section #1, along with your ages and address. After the words *who are the*, type in either *maternal* or *paternal*, whichever describes you.

3. In section #3, fill in the information for your grandchildren.

4. In sections #4 and #5, type in the parents' names and addresses.

5. In the last paragraph in section #8, your names go on the first line after the word *Grandparents*, and the specific visitation schedule you want goes on the line after the word *from*.

6. This form then needs to be signed by you (and your spouse if he or she is joining in the petition) on the lines after the word "by."

PETITION OF
GRANDPARENT(S)
FOR INTERVENTION
IN SUIT AFFECTING
THE PARENT-CHILD
RELATIONSHIP
(FORM 5)

Form 5 is for use in Texas if there is already a divorce or other lawsuit involving custody or visitation. (For an example of this form completed, see form C in appendix B.) To complete:

1. Since you are intervening in an ongoing lawsuit, use the heading from that lawsuit.

2. The first line in the introductory (unnumbered) paragraph is for your name (and your spouse's name if you are both filing).

3. In section #1, the first four blanks are for the name and age of you and your spouse. The fifth blank should be completed by filling in either *paternal* or *maternal*, as appropriate. The final blank in this section is for your address.

4. In section #3, fill in the blanks for each grandchild with whom you seek visitation.

5. In sections #4 and #5, type in the parents' names and addresses.

6. In section #6, the form assumes that no other persons have any court-ordered relationships with your grandchildren. However, if some third party or agency has been awarded legal rights to the child (temporary legal custody, for example), you will need to change this section to reflect those relationships.

7. In the last paragraph in section #8, your names go on the line after the word *Grandparents*, and the specific visitation schedule you want goes on the line after the word *from*.

8. This form then needs to be signed by you (and your spouse if he or she is joining in the petition) on the lines after the word *by*.

9. In the Certificate of Service section, fill in the names of the other parties and the date you sent them copies of your petition. This should be the same day you filed the petition. If you are modifying this form for use outside of Texas, you will need to check the laws of your state to see if you need to do something more than send the parties copies by certified mail. For more information about formal notification to other parties, see chapter 7.

REQUEST FOR MEDIATION

The Request for Mediation (form 11) in appendix C is the form used in Missouri, but it may also be used to request mediation in other states that have provisions for mediation after a lawsuit has been filed. To complete form 11:

1. Complete the case style portion of the form according to the information in the previous section of this chapter.

2. In the first paragraph type in your name on the first line. On all of the other lines in the three main paragraphs, type in the word *Plaintiff, Petitioner,* or *Movant,* whichever term is used in your state.

3. Sign your name on the *signature* line, and type in your name, address, and telephone number on the lines indicated. File this with the court clerk. The judge will fill in the order portion of the form.

COURT PROCEDURES

After you complete your complaint or petition, you will need to file it with the court, notify the other parties, prepare for and attend a court hearing, and prepare an order for the judge to sign after he or she makes a decision. See chapter 7 for information about the procedures to follow once your complaint or petition is completed.

NOTIFYING THE OTHER PARTIES

After you have completed your complaint or petition, you will need to notify the other parties involved (usually the parents) that you are filing court papers for visitation. See the section in chapter 7, titled "Notifying Others" for more information about notification.

AFTER THE COURT ORDER

After you have been to court and have been successful in convincing the judge to grant you visitation, you are all set to begin enjoying regular time with your grandchildren. Ideally, this turns out to be a very stable situation for the grandchild with a minimum of conflict between the parents and grandparents. This enables the grandchild to have the many and varied benefits of a close relationship with his or her grandparents. In this situation, the parents get to be parents and the grandparents get to enjoy being grandparents. Sometimes, though, the family situation does not work out this way, and you, as grandparents, may find yourselves facing the decision to seek custody of your grandchildren.

SHOULD YOU FILE FOR CUSTODY? 4

Over the past ten to fifteen years, the number of grandparents rearing their grandchildren has risen dramatically. A 1990 *Time Magazine* article reports that three million children live with their grandparents, an increase of fifty percent since 1980. Approximately 882,000 of these three million live away from their parents. Most commonly, those parents are absent as a result of drug or alcohol abuse, making them either unable or unwilling to parent their own children. Other factors influencing the rising rate of grandparents rearing their grandchildren include the divorce rate and the economy. Many parents, especially single parents, are unable to afford to care for their children. Sometimes, abuse by a parent or stepparent is a factor that prompts grandparents to seek custody of their grandchildren.

QUALIFYING TO FILE FOR CUSTODY

Just as grandparent visitation statutes establish prerequisites for visitation, the states have requirements that grandparents must meet in order to obtain legal custody. In order to have standing to seek custody in most states, you will have to establish that you have had significant past contacts with your grandchild. Assuming that the parents appear in court and contest your attempt to get custody, the greatest hurdle you will have to overcome is the parental preference. In the overwhelming majority of states, the court starts out presuming that the parents should have custody. The burden is on the grandparents to overcome that presumption. Various states use different words and phrases to describe what it takes to overcome that burden, but generally you must prove that the parents are unfit in order to take custody from them. In states that do not have the parental preference, the "best interest of the child" is the determining factor. Regardless of the standard used by your state, there may be a number of reasons or situations which will cause you to consider filing a lawsuit to get custody of your grandchildren.

REASONS TO CONSIDER FILING FOR CUSTODY

ABUSIVE OR NEGLECTFUL PARENTS

In today's society, there are more reported cases of abuse and neglect than ever before. Sometimes, this is a reflection of drug or alcohol addiction. There are, however, many other causes of abuse. Addicted parents may leave their children with the grandparents, forcing them to seek custody. In other cases, the grandparents may become the primary caregivers for their grandchildren as a result of action by a child welfare agency. Often, a grandparent may become aware of instances of abuse or neglect on their own, and decide to seek custody in order to protect their grandchildren.

Regardless of how the grandparents become involved in custody litigation relating to abuse or neglect, a contested custody suit of this nature is likely to be very messy. Most parents who invest the time and money to contest a custody case will vigorously deny that they have abused or neglected their children, especially if the possibility of criminal charges stemming from the abuse or neglect exists. Physical abuse can be difficult to prove unless there are injuries that could only be the result of abuse, which are documented by third persons. For example, a scar or bruise in the shape of a coiled extension cord is difficult to explain as anything other than abuse; a black eye is subject to many explanations. Sexual abuse is even more difficult to prove. There is rarely any physical evidence of sexual abuse of children. In fact, the only evidence may be the testimony of the child.

Very young children are not legally competent to testify. Older children, although allowed to testify, are easily confused about dates, times, and sequencing of events. Children are also easily suggestible as they tend to be eager to please, and their allegations of sexual abuse are often countered by the *coaching defense*. The coaching defense involves claims by the alleged abuser that some adult, usually the person bringing forward the allegation, has coached or manipulated the child into saying he or she has been sexually abused. Undertaking a case of this nature is a very serious endeavor. It requires a major investment of time and money, even if you represent yourself, and is difficult to handle without a lawyer. There is also the very real possibility that if you are unable to convince a judge or jury that the abuse has occurred, you will be totally excluded from the lives of your grandchildren. In spite of those odds, it is also difficult to stand by and do nothing if you have reason to believe that your grandchildren are being abused.

Neglect is also difficult to prove as there may not be much evidence other than the testimony of family members, many of whom will not want to take sides in a custody fight. The testimony of family members is also more easily attacked than that of disinterested third parties, especially when there is little or no physical evidence to back the claim. In some cases, however, third party evidence will be available. For instance, if the police or child welfare investigators are called in because the children have been left alone somewhere, you will have the testimony of the police officers or investigators to help your case.

If you are able to establish the existence of abuse or neglect, this will be sufficient in most instances to show that the parents are unfit. This alone, however, will not entitle you to custody. You will also have to convince the judge or jury of your fitness as custodians and show that awarding custody to you is in the best interest of your grandchildren. There may be problems in proving these matters to the satisfaction of the court. Some of the obstacles will be discussed later.

UNSTABLE
PARENTS

Another situation which may give rise to a custody fight is when the parents are unstable. Instability can refer to a number of situations within the family. A family may be financially unstable or emotionally unstable. When taken in conjunction with the laws of the particular state, the nature and severity of the financial instability determine whether or not a grandparent can get custody. For example, if the financial instability involves frequent job and residence changes, that alone will not be enough for a nonparent to get custody in most states. However, if the financial instability means that the child is living in substandard housing without the basic necessities, the grandparents stand a much better chance of having enough evidence to win. The same may be said of emotional stability. Particularly in states where the parents have a statutory preference for custody of their children, it will take a significant amount of instability to defeat the presumption. The presence of significant instability is a factor that triggers an evaluation of whether or not a grandparent should seek custody of the grandchildren.

ABSENT
PARENTS

Parents may be absent from their children's lives for a number of reasons. The most obvious reason for a parent to be absent is death. Once again, the drug and alcohol abuse problem impacts the family situation. An addicted parent may leave his or her child with the grandparents and vanish from the scene. No matter what the reason for the absentee parents, this situation will likely force a grandparent into court to seek custody. In that instance, the grandparents will need custody for legal reasons, such as to consent to medical care and to enroll the child in school. The basic problems involved in a contested custody case do not apply in this situation as the absent parents are not likely to be in court contesting the change of custody to the grandparents.

OBSTACLES TO GETTING CUSTODY

AGE

When the parent does contest the custody case, there are some significant obstacles facing the grandparents. One difficulty a grandparent may encounter is age. One of the factors a court considers in making a custody determination is long term stability of the child's situation. All other things being equal, a younger grandparent will have an advantage over an older one. Whether accurate or not, an older grandparent is at something of a disadvantage. Especially where the custody of younger children is involved, the court will question the remaining life span of older grandparents; health problems, either existing or potential, are also a factor the courts use in the custody equation. The judge will wonder whether the older grandparent will be physically able to care for the child until the child reaches adulthood. This is the reason the younger, healthier grandparent has an edge over a grandparent who is older or who has health problems.

YOUR TRACK
RECORD AS A
PARENT

A second factor in the custody equation is the grandparents' track record as parents. If you are competing against your son or daughter for custody of your grandchild, you should expect your son or daughter to bring up every mistake you ever made as a parent. If the discipline methods you employed as a parent would be considered abusive by today's standards, you will have a disadvantage to overcome, regardless of the methods you use to discipline the grandchild. If you were a largely absent parent who left your own children mostly with other relatives or sitters, this fact will count against you in the eyes of the judge or jury. On the other hand, if there is not any negative evidence, or only minor negative evidence, this can be an advantage for you.

YOUR
RELATIONSHIP
WITH YOUR
OWN CHILDREN

A third potential disadvantage to grandparents seeking custody is the current state of their relationships with their own children. A grandparent who has a poor or nonexistent relationship with some or all of his or her children will be at a significant disadvantage when compared to a grandparent with good relationships with all of his or her children. Another issue contained within the overall parent-child relationship is the grandparent's motivation for seeking custody of a grandchild. Are you filing because you still feel the need to control your son's or daughter's life? Are you filing to fulfill some maternal or paternal need of your own? Are you filing because you wish you were your grandchild's parent? A "yes" answer to any of these questions indicates that you should reevaluate the need to file in light of your motivation for filing. Filing to punish your son or daughter for some affront or misdeed is also not well-considered.

YOUR
FINANCIAL
SITUATION

Your financial situation may also become an obstacle in a contested custody case. Another of the many factors that goes into a determination of what is in the child's best interest is the ability to meet the financial needs of the child. Everyone recognizes that rearing a child is an expensive proposition. Many grandparents will find themselves in the position of being on a fixed income. With costs rising every year, your income may not be sufficient to take on the expenses of caring for your grandchild. While this issue may not be the one that solely determines the outcome of your case, it is something that may make a difference in a close case.

PARENTAL
PREFERENCE

Another factor involved in custody disputes is one that has been previously mentioned. That factor is the law of parental preference. This obstacle is one that should not be taken lightly. Even if you are fairly young, healthy, financially secure grandparents with a wonderful record as parents or grandparents, and if you could easily prevail in a state where the only test is the best interest of the child, you may not be able to get custody in a state with a parental preference. This law, by itself, may be enough to keep you from getting custody of your grandchild. The parental preference is stronger in some states than in others and you will need to determine the strength as well as the existence of this policy. Before you file a lawsuit for custody, you need to evaluate the evidence you will be able to use in court in light of the presumption favoring the parents in custody cases. To determine whether or not the parental preference applies in your state, check the listing for your state in appendix A of this book.

Grounds

The qualifications for obtaining custody are not as specific as those for visitation. Once you have reviewed your status in light of the parental preference and have decided to seek custody, the next standard you will run into is the "best interest of the child." Some states simply state this general concept, while other states have specific statutory guidelines for determining the best interest. Typical of these guidelines is §25.24.150 of the Alaska Statutes, which includes the following:

> ...the physical, emotional, religious, and social needs of the child; the capability and desire of each parent to meet these needs; the child's preference if the child is sufficient age and capacity to form a preference; the love and affection existing between the child and each parent; the length of time the child has lived in a stable, satisfactory environment and the desirability of maintaining continuity; the desire and ability of each parent to allow an open and loving frequent relationship between the child and the other parent; any evidence of domestic violence, child abuse, or child neglect in the proposed custodial household or a history of violence between the parents; evidence that substance abuse by either parent or other member of the household directly affects the emotional or physical well-being of the child; and other factors that the court considers pertinent.

Even if your state does not have specific guidelines included in its statutes, the above guidelines will be similar to what courts in your state will consider as part of the best interest standard. As a reminder, if the parties reside in different states, the provisions of the Uniform Child Custody Jurisdiction Act will also apply.

Uniform Child Custody Jurisdiction Act

As noted before, the Uniform Child Custody Jurisdiction Act (UCCJA) is a law designed to avoid conflicts between courts of different states in child custody situations. All fifty states and the District of Columbia have enacted some version of this law, and most provisions will be the same in every state. However, before you file anything in a case in which the UCCJA is involved, be sure to check the laws for your state, as it is possible for state legislatures to make modifications to the provisions.

Generally, the courts in a particular state can hear a child custody case in any of the following situations:

1. If that state is the home state of the child on the date the legal proceeding began.

2. If that state has been the child's home state within six months of that date the legal proceeding began.

3. If the child has been removed from that state by someone and a parent continues to live in the state.

4. If the child and at least one parent have a significant connection with that state, other than mere physical presence in the state.

5. If the child is physically present in the state and has either been abandoned or is in danger of being abused or neglected.

6. If another state has deferred to your state.

If you otherwise qualify for a court in your state to hear a custody case, the court can still refuse to hear your case. One reason for this refusal might be that another proceeding concerning custody of the child was already on file in another state. Another reason might be that your state's court decides that it is an "inconvenient forum." In making this determination, the court will consider the best interest of the child, the connections the child and his family have to other states, and the availability of substantial evidence in the other state. If you have wrongfully taken the child from another state or engaged in "similar reprehensible conduct," a state can also decline to exercise jurisdiction.

UNIFORM CHILD CUSTODY JURISDICTION ACT AFFIDAVIT (FORM 6)

Assuming your state can hear your custody case, there are some specific provisions in the UCCJA with which you must comply. The most important of these relates to information that must be provided to the court in or with the first document you file. This information must be provided in the form of an affidavit. Form 6 in appendix C is a Uniform Child Custody Jurisdiction Act Affidavit, which can be used if you can't find a specific form for your state. Some states require a form like this to be filed in all domestic relations cases involving children, if for no other reason than to assure the judge that the UCCJA does not apply. Some states may allow the same information to be included in the petition. The court clerk may be able to tell you if you need to file such an affidavit.

The UCCJA Affidavit requires very specific information. To complete:

1. Complete the case style portion exactly the same as in your complaint or petition.

2. The child's name and present address (#1);

3. The places where the child has lived within the last five years (#2);

4. The names and present addresses of the persons with whom the child has lived during that period (#3);

5. Whether the party has participated (as a party, witness, or in any other capacity) in any other litigation concerning the child (#4);

6. Whether the party has any information of any other pending proceedings relating to the child (#5);

7. Whether the party knows of any other person not already a party to the lawsuit who has physical custody of the child or claims to have custody or visitation rights with respect to the child (#6).

It is important to remember that if any of the above information changes or you become aware of new information, you must provide that information to the court.

There are also provisions applicable to the recognition of court orders from other states and the enforcement and modification of those orders. If you are trying to change an order from another state or enforce such an order, you will need to familiarize yourself with these provisions. For example, you must first register the out-of-state order in your new state before it can be enforced or modified. You will need a certified copy of this order to get it properly registered in the new state.

FILING FOR CUSTODY 5

In order to obtain custody of your grandchildren, you will have to file pleadings in court. (*Pleadings* are simply documents filed with the court.) The exact documents you will file depends on the status of any legal proceedings between the parents. If there have been previous proceedings between the parents and a court has entered an order for custody of the children, you will need to file a lawsuit to modify the custody order. If the parents are in the process of divorcing or obtaining a legal separation, you will be filing an intervention in the proceedings between the parents. If there have been no custody orders entered by the court, you will file an original lawsuit.

PREPARING YOUR PETITION

LEGAL FORMS
In all cases, you initiate the legal proceedings by filing some sort of initial pleading. It will usually be called a *complaint* or a *petition*. These documents vary depending on the type of case and type of proceeding. Everything that you file with the court should be typed and double spaced. Some states require that documents be filed on legal-sized paper, some states require letter-size. You can find out what the requirements for your state are by asking the court clerk. All documents have a heading called the *case style*. Case styles vary from state to state. To

find out what form is appropriate for your state, ask the clerk to let you see a pending case file or look in a form book in your law library. Generally, the style will contain the name of the state, county, and the court designation (*13th District Court*, for example), as well as the names of the parties.

There will also be a *docket* or *case number* assigned to your case. If you are intervening in a pending divorce case, the docket number for your pleadings will be the docket number assigned to the divorce case. If you are filing a new lawsuit, leave a blank space for the number on your first pleading. The clerk will assign you a number when you file the pleading. Use that number for all future filings in that case.

Just before the body of your petition should be the title of the document. Refer to the forms included in appendix B. They have titles like *Petition in Intervention* and *Complaint for Child Custody*. All your documents should have titles like this, and the title will vary depending on what you are filing. Visit your law library, or look at a case at the court clerk's office, to find out what title to use. Some states use the word *Complaint*; whereas others use the word *Petition*. Similarly, some states use the words *Plaintiff* and *Defendant*; whereas others use *Petitioner* and *Respondent*. Some may even use *Petitioner* and *Defendant*.

A typical case style might be as follows:

```
                    STATE OF MICHIGAN
          SIXTEENTH JUDICIAL CIRCUIT, MACOMB COUNTY

JOHN DOE and JANE DOE,

            Plaintiffs,

VS.                              CASE NO._____

ROBERT DOE and WANDA DOE,

            Defendants.

             COMPLAINT FOR CHILD CUSTODY
```

At the end of your pleadings, you should close with a paragraph telling the judge what it is you want him or her to do. For example, see paragraph 4 of the Complaint/Petition for Child Custody, found in appendix B as form I. Additionally, you should always sign your documents and then type in your name, address, and phone number. Some states have fill-in-the-blank forms or "check off" forms. Before you begin preparing this paperwork, check with the court clerk to see if they have forms available. If they do, use the forms from the clerk.

COMPLAINT/
PETITION FOR
CHILD CUSTODY
(FORM 15)

Form 15 is for use in all states except Texas. Before using this form, look at specific forms tailored to meet the requirements of your state. Then modify this form as necessary. (For a filled-in example of this form, see form I in appendix B.) To complete:

1. Complete the case style portion of the form according to the information in the previous section of this chapter. Follow the language and format commonly used in your state and county.

2. In the first (unnumbered) paragraph, fill in the names of the grandparents seeking custody on the first line. The second line (after the phrase *hereinafter called the...*) is for your designation as a party; your state will likely use either *Plaintiff*, *Petitioner*, or *Movant*. In the third line, type in the word *Complaint*, or *Petition*, or whatever word or phrase you used as a title. In the fourth line, type in the name or names of the parents (the same person or persons listed as defendants or respondents in the case style). The fifth line is for the parents' party designation, which will be either *Defendant* or *Respondent*.

3. Paragraph #1 is to identify the relationship of all of the parties. On the first line, type in your designation as a party (*Plaintiff*, *Petitioner*, or *Movant*). On the second line, type in either *maternal grandparents* or *paternal grandparents*, whichever applies to you. Type your address on the third line. The next two lines are for the parents' designation as parties (*Defendants* or *Respondents*), and their address. If they are living apart, list both addresses (see form A in appendix B for an example of this). In the last two lines type in the names of the children (your state may also require their ages or birth dates to be listed; if you

aren't sure, you may want to include them just to be safe), and their current address.

4. Paragraph #2 is for you to state the legal *grounds* for why you are entitled to custody. The first blank in the grounds section should contain either your name or your party designation (*Plaintiff, Petitioner,* or *Movant*). The second blank is where you describe the facts (using the factors from your state statute) which you believe justify your request for visitation. Be sure to read the listing for your state in appendix A, and consult your state's custody statutes before filling in this space. It is a good idea to use the language of your state's custody statute as closely as possible, and include a summary of the facts which indicate that custody should be changed. For example, the listing for Illinois in appendix A indicates that the custody statute may be found in section 31-1-11 of the Annotated Indiana Code (this is the notation "A.I.C. §31-1-11 et seq."). If you look up section 31-1-11.5-21, you would find that custody is to be determined by what is in the child's best interest, considering the following factors:

   1. the age and sex of the child;

   2. the wishes of the parents and the child;

   3. the interaction and interrelationship between the child and the parents, siblings, and other significant persons;

   4. the child's adjustment to home, school, and community; and

   5. any special educational or medical needs of the child.

   You would want to relate your grandchild's situation to as many of these five factors as possible to show why he or she would be better off with you. For example: *The child has expressed a desire to live with the petitioners, has had substantial past interaction with the petitioners, and has not adjusted well to his new school since his parents' divorce and could return to his original school if in the petitioners' custody.* However, to overcome the presumption that a child is best off in the custody of his or her parent, in most states you would have to show that your grandchild is suffering, or is likely to suffer, harm if he remains with his parents. This usually would require additional statements claiming some kind of abuse, neglect, or some type of improper home environment.

5. Paragraph #3 tells the court whether there are any other cases pending which relate to visitation. If there are no such cases, type in the word *none* in the space after this paragraph. If there is another case, type in the case style from that other case (name of the court, names of parties, and case number).

6. Paragraph #4 is for you to tell the judge what you are asking him or her to do. The first line in the relief section is for your name or party designation (*Plaintiff, Petitioner,* or *Movant*). On the second line, fill in exactly what you want the judge to order with regard to custody. See form I in appendix B for an example of how this might be completed.

7. Fill in the date, sign your name, and fill in the name, address, and telephone number information on the appropriate lines.

ORIGINAL PETITION
IN SUIT AFFECTING
PARENT-CHILD
RELATIONSHIP
(FORM 16)

Form 16 is for use in Texas where there is no divorce or other lawsuit pending which involves custody or visitation. This form is fairly self-explanatory as to what information needs to be filled in on each line. (For an example of this form completed, see form J in appendix B.) This form may be adapted to other states, but you will need to change the legal term for custody. In Texas, primary custody is called *managing conservatorship*, but in other states this will be referred to by some other term or phrase, such as *physical custody, legal custody,* or perhaps just *custody*. You can review form 16 for additional guidance, but you will also need to look at specific forms tailored to meet the requirements of your state. To complete:

1. In the case style section, type in the number of the court district and the name of the county. Leave the case number line blank— the clerk will assign the number. The grandchildren's names go

in the space just below the words *in the interest of*, and in section #3. Obviously, the rest of the blanks in #3 apply to the grandchildren as well.

2. Your names go in section #1 along with your address.

3. In section #4, type in the parents' names and addresses.

4. In section #7, type in the names of the parent or parents you believe should pay child support.

5. This form then needs to be signed by you (and your spouse if he or she is joining in the petition) on the lines after the word *by*.

PETITION FOR INTERVENTION IN SUIT AFFECTING THE PARENT-CHILD RELATIONSHIP (FORM 17)

Form 17 is for use in Texas where there is already a divorce or other lawsuit involving custody or visitation. Form 17 will be completed the same as form 16, except that the case style will be exactly the same as the case in which you are intervening. Also, in the certificate of service, fill in the names of the other parties and the date you sent them copies of your petition. This should be the same day you file the petition. If you are modifying this form for use outside of Texas, you will need to check the laws of your state to see if you need to do something more than send the parties copies by certified mail. For more information about formal notification to other parties, see chapter 7.

FINANCIAL AFFIDAVIT (FORM 26)

Some states may require you to file a financial statement. The two main purposes for this would be to show that you have the financial ability to care for your grandchild, and for the court to determine the amount of child support the parents should pay to you. If your state or court requires a financial statement, you may need to use an official form provided by the court clerk or some other state agency. If a financial statement is required, but there is no official form, you can use form 26 in appendix C. Just fill in the required information on each line.

COURT PROCEDURES

After you complete your complaint or petition, you will need to file your papers with the court; notify the other parties; prepare for and attend a court hearing; and prepare an order for the judge to sign after he or she makes a decision. See chapter 7 for information about the procedures to follow once your complaint or petition is completed.

NOTIFYING THE OTHER PARTIES

After you have completed your complaint or petition, you will need to notify the other parties involved (usually the parents) that you are filing court papers for visitation. See the section entitled "Notifying Others" in chapter 7 for more information about notification.

Once you have your pleadings filed, you will have to begin preparing your evidence. A more thorough discussion of what you will need in the way of evidence will be found in chapter 8. However, you may find the idea of representing yourself in court intimidating. You may even be considering hiring a lawyer. Therefore, the following chapter will evaluate the pros and cons of hiring a lawyer and will contain some tips for selecting an attorney.

ROLE OF THE LAWYER 6

ADVANTAGES OF HIRING A LAWYER

As with anything, there are advantages and disadvantages to hiring a lawyer to represent you in court. The advantages are fairly obvious. An attorney knows the law and the procedural rules; these are both things you will be responsible for knowing just as if you were a lawyer if you choose to represent yourself. The lawyer also has experience in trying custody and visitation cases. He or she will know what evidence will play favorably in front of the judge or jury and what evidence will hurt your chances of victory.

Another advantage is that the lawyer has objectivity. You are a party to the case, and, as such, have a big emotional investment in the outcome. There are also likely to be emotions involving the other parties at play. No matter what emotional strategies are employed by the other parties, your lawyer will be able to help you maintain perspective and make decisions regarding your case with a clearer head and distance from the emotional issues. Also, you may be taken more seriously if you are represented by an attorney. A final advantage of using a lawyer is that you do not have to be responsible for all of the administrative details that go along with a lawsuit.

ADVANTAGES OF REPRESENTING YOURSELF

Of course, this freedom from details comes at a price. Cost is the most obvious advantage to representing yourself. Most lawyers will charge you an hourly rate, and probably require you to make a deposit in advance, to handle a custody or visitation case. The hourly rate will vary depending on your geographical location and the experience of the lawyer. You should always receive an itemized bill from your lawyer so that you know how your money is being spent. A second advantage to representing yourself is the ability to keep your case moving. Most attorneys handle a heavy caseload, and sometimes work on your case will come behind more pressing demands of other cases.

TIPS FOR SELECTING A LAWYER

If you decide the disadvantages of representing yourself outweigh the advantages, you will face the problem of deciding which lawyer to hire. It is important that you hire an attorney who is knowledgeable about domestic relations cases; it is also important that you feel comfortable with that lawyer. If you do not already know a good family law attorney, there are several sources of referrals. One of the best ways to find a lawyer is through someone you know. Ask around to get names from acquaintances of lawyers they have dealt with and liked. You can also call the local bar association. Most, especially in larger towns and cities, maintain referral services. Of course, you can also check the telephone book. Feel free to schedule consultations with more than one attorney. Some will give you a free initial consultation; others will charge you. You should be able to find out what the charge will be for the consultation when you schedule the appointment. When you meet with the attorney, do not hesitate to ask the lawyer about his or her educational background and experience. You should also come away from your initial consultation knowing how the lawyer intends to handle your case and what you can expect during the course of your lawsuit. You should feel comfortable with that person and have confidence in him or her. And remember: If at any time you become dissatisfied with your lawyer, you can always discharge that lawyer and hire another.

Once you have made the decision to hire an attorney, there are several things you can do to make the experience better. One of the keys to a good relationship with your attorney is to understand what is going on with your case and the law that applies to the case. If you do not understand something, keep asking questions until you do understand. The law can be complicated and you should not be embarrassed if you don't understand something the first time. Your lawyer should be willing to take whatever time is necessary to answer your questions.

It is also important that you tell your lawyer everything that might apply to your case. It is much better to let your lawyer decide what is important; things that may not seem important to you may be very important. If you withhold information because it is damaging, your lawyer will not have an opportunity to minimize the damage to you if he or she hears that information for the first time in court. Remember, anything you tell your lawyer is confidential and cannot be revealed without your consent.

Another key to being satisfied with the way your case is handled is to be realistic. In many more instances than you may realize going in, the system is not going to work the way you think it should. The law may not seem fair to you. These are things over which your lawyer has no control and being angry with your attorney accomplishes nothing except to damage the working relationship between the two of you. When you find yourself in that situation, do not vent your frustration on your lawyer; instead, accept the situation and do your best to work with your attorney within the system to get the best outcome you can.

You will also need to be patient. Our legal system will often move at a frustratingly slow pace. In many places, the courts are very busy and it may take a long time before your case can be heard. There is nothing your lawyer can do about these scheduling problems, and your relationship with your attorney will be much better if you refrain from demanding that he or she schedule things on your schedule instead of the court's. You will also need to be patient with your attorney. You are not the only client your lawyer has, and it is unrealistic to expect your lawyer to always be available for you. Lawyers who handle family law cases spend a significant amount of time in court. When in court, lawyers give their undivided attention to that client, and will have to return your calls at another time. When your time in court comes, you will expect that same treatment. So you will need to understand when your lawyer takes several hours, or maybe even a day or more, to return your call.

When these things happen, talking to the secretary can be a big help. There are many questions that the secretary can answer for you. This enables you to get the information you need without talking to the attorney. You should talk to the secretary whenever possible and leave information with her instead of waiting to talk to your lawyer. Another benefit to this is that you won't be billed for talking to the secretary.

It is also important that you not become a pest. When you need information from you lawyer or need to pass information to him or her, call. Be organized when you call: get your questions answered, find out what happens next and when you should expect to hear something and finish your call. Don't make frequent unnecessary phone calls to your lawyer, as this just runs up your bill and irritates your lawyer. You should also be on time—both for appointments and for court settings.

Pay your bill on time. The clients who get the most prompt attention are those that pay their bills on time. While you should review your bill carefully and be sure you understand the fee agreement, you should expect to pay for everything the attorney does on your case. This includes more than just going to court for you; you will also be billed for paperwork, letters, and telephone calls.

Even with a lawyer representing you, you will need to provide him or her with the information necessary to prepare the case. While each case is different and will require different evidence, there are some general types of evidence and witnesses that you will need in most contested custody and visitation cases.

COURT PROCEDURE 7

FILING YOUR PETITION

Before you take your petition to the court, call the clerk and ask what the filing fee is and what forms of payment the court will accept. Then take your original pleading and several copies to the clerk's office. (In addition to the original for the court clerk, you will need at least one copy for each party, and a file-stamped copy for yourself.) Tell the clerk you want to file the petition, and then follow whatever instructions he or she gives you.

In most states you will need more than just your complaint or petition. Unless you are filing against parties to an existing case, and your state allows some other notice procedure, you will need a summons form to go with your petition. Most states have their own summons form, so use the one for the state where you will be filing. Often, the court clerk can provide the official summons form. Many states also have a *cover sheet* which must be filed with each new case. A cover sheet usually just provides the court with statistical information for use by the court in compiling data for budgeting and other internal purposes. These forms are usually provided by the court clerk.

In some states, you will need to file certain affidavits. You will need to do some research to find out what is required in your state. Sometimes you won't find out about what else needs to be filed until you try to file your petition. The clerk will tell you what form is missing. You will then need to find a copy of the required form, complete it, and return to the clerk to file your case. Several forms for different situations are provided in appendix C, with some sample completed forms in appendix B. There are three main places to look for forms you need but don't have: 1) the clerk's office may provide forms; 2) a file in another case at the clerk's office may reveal the needed form; and 3) a form book at your local law library may contain the form you need.

NOTIFYING OTHERS

When you file a complaint or petition for visitation or custody there are certain people you must notify. In every case, you must notify the other people with legal relationships to the minor children. In most cases, you will just have to notify the parents. But, if the child welfare authorities are involved, or some other nonparent has been to court and has a court-ordered relationship, these people must all also be notified. This notification procedure is called *service of process*.

Each state has its own rules for how *process* (i.e., court paper) is to be *served* (i.e., delivered), and you should check with the rules of civil procedure for your state to decide how this is to be accomplished. It may be that a sheriff or constable has to personally deliver the papers to the other party, or you may be able to mail the documents by certified mail. It is important to check these rules carefully. Using a method that is not authorized by your state will mean that the judge cannot hear your case until you have gone back and served the lawsuit properly.

WAIVER
(FORM 12)

If you know at the time you file your lawsuit that your case will settle, you may be able to have the other parties sign a notarized waiver of service. A waiver form is included as form 12 in appendix C. (For an example of a completed waiver, see form G in appendix B.) One warning: the waiver must be signed after the original pleading has been filed. A waiver signed before the lawsuit is filed is invalid. If both parents are willing to sign, have each of them complete a separate form. To complete:

1. Complete the case style portion according to the instructions in the section in chapter 3 or chapter 5 titled "Legal Forms."

2. Type in the name of your state and county after the words *state of* and *county of*.

3. On the line in the first paragraph, type in the name of the person (usually one of the parents) who will be signing this form.

4. On the first line in the second paragraph, type in the word *Defendant* or *Respondent*, whichever applies in your state. Type the address of the person who will be signing this form on the second line of this paragraph, and on the third line type in the title of the complaint or petition (*Complaint for Child Custody*, *Petition for Grandparent Visitation*, etc.).

5. Have the person sign the form before a notary public. This form will then be filed with the court clerk.

SUMMONS   In some states you will need to arrange for service by the sheriff, and in others the court clerk will do this. If the clerk arranges for service, he or she will need a copy of the complaint or petition for every person who is going to be served, and you will need one or two copies for yourself.

The form of the *Summons*, which is the official notification of the lawsuit that will be attached to your complaint or petition, varies from state to state. In many states, this form will be furnished and prepared by the court clerk. Before you go to the courthouse to file your lawsuit, ask the clerk whether or not you have to provide a summons. If you need to provide one, look in a form book or a pending file and copy the form. Form E in appendix B is an example of a completed Summons, so you can get an idea of what one looks like. However, you must use the Summons form which is acceptable in your state.

After delivering the papers, the sheriff will file a document with the court verifying who was served and when. Anyone being served with a complaint or petition will have a certain number of days in which to file a written response with the court.

CERTIFICATE OF SERVICE (FORM 7)

Once the other parties have been legally served with your petition, you will also need to send them copies of any other papers you may file with the court later. This is usually done by regular first-class mail, although you may also hand-deliver them (however, a subpoena for someone to appear for a hearing or deposition, or to produce documents, must be personally served; so don't use a Certificate of Service form for a subpoena). To show the court that you have mailed copies of these later papers to the other parties, you need to complete a Certificate of Service. This can either be at the end of the document you are filing, or on a separate sheet of paper. Form 7 in appendix C is a Certificate of Service form. To complete:

1. Complete the case style portion according to the instructions in the section of chapter 3 or chapter 5 titled "Legal Forms."

2. Type in the name or title of the papers being sent on the first line in the main paragraph.

3. Check the appropriate blank for how the papers are being sent (*mailed*, or *hand delivered*), and fill in the date the papers are sent or delivered.

4. Type in the name, address, and telephone number of the person (or persons) to whom the papers are being sent or delivered (usually the parents or their attorney).

5. Sign your name on the line marked *signature*, and type in your name, address, and telephone number on the appropriate lines below. This form can be attached to whatever form you are sending, and filed with the court.

NOTICE OF
HEARING
(FORM 10)

Basically, a Notice of Hearing simply includes the case style, the name of the party (or his or her attorney) being notified, the type of hearing being held, and the date, time, and place of the hearing. Form 10 is a Notice of Hearing form which can be used for trial or any other type of hearing. This form may need to be modified to comply with the requirements of your court. (For an example of a completed form, see form L in appendix B.)

MOTION TO SET
HEARING
(FORM 28)

In some states you can simply call the court clerk or the judge's secretary and obtain a hearing date. Then you just mail or deliver a Notice of Hearing to the other party (or attorney) and show up at the hearing. In other states you will need to file a Motion to Set Hearing. This is simply a more formal way of asking for a hearing. If you need to file a motion, try to get a form either from the court clerk or from a form book at your local law library. If you can't find one specific for your state, you can use form 28 in appendix C. To complete:

1. Complete the case style portion according to the instructions in the section of chapter 3 or chapter 5 entitled "Legal Forms."

2. Type in either *Plaintiff*, *Petitioner*, or *Movant*, whichever term is used in your state, on the first line in the main paragraph.

3. Type in either *child visitation* or *child custody* on the second line in the main paragraph.

4. Type in the date and your name, address, and telephone number on the appropriate lines, then sign on the line marked *signature* and file it with the court clerk. Be sure to mail a copy of this form to the other parties, and complete and file a Certificate of Service (Form 7) showing that you have sent out copies.

WHEN YOU CAN'T LOCATE THE PARENT

Your daughter and her husband have divorced. He left the state three years ago to avoid paying child support, and no one knows where he is now. Your daughter asks you to babysit for your granddaughter for a few hours while she goes shopping. Your daughter calls two days later to tell you that she can't take it anymore as a single parent, and she won't be back until she gets her head straight. Plus, she won't tell you where she is. So here you are with your eight-year-old granddaughter who needs to be enrolled in school. And what if she needs medical treatment? This, or something very similar, is not an uncommon scenario in today's world. An infinite number of circumstances can result in you not knowing the whereabouts of one or both of your grandchild's parents.

If you need to file for custody, or visitation, and can't locate one or both of the parents, you won't be able to notify them of your petition by any of the means discussed above. You will then need to use an alternative method of service. In such situations the law provides for what is known as *service by publication*. This is where you publish a notice of your lawsuit in a newspaper. This can be a very tricky procedure, which varies greatly from state to state, so you will need to either consult a lawyer and do some research at your local law library.

DEFAULT JUDGMENTS

Once your complaint or petition has been served correctly, the other parties will have a deadline for filing a response with the court to contest your lawsuit. If the deadline passes and the other parties do not file responses, you will be able to get a default judgment. The usual procedure is for you to file a Motion for Default (form 8) with the court clerk. The clerk then issues a Default (which may be included in the motion form or may be a separate document), and you submit an order for the judge to sign. Some states may not allow a default in custody or visitation cases, and may require you to set a hearing and present evidence to support what you want. Others may require a short hearing on the default. The court clerk should be willing to tell you what the default procedures are in your court.

MOTION FOR
DEFAULT
(FORM 8)

A Motion for Default form is included in appendix C as form 8. This form may need to be modified to comply with the requirements of your court. (For an example of a completed Motion for Default, see form F in appendix B.) To complete:

1. Complete the case style portion according to the instructions in the section of chapter 3 or chapter 5 entitled "Legal Forms."

2. On the first line in the main paragraph, type in *Plaintiff*, *Petitioner*, or *Movant*, whichever is used in your state. On the second line type in the name of the Defendant(s)/Respondent(s) you wish to have a default entered against. In other words, if one parent responded to your petition and the other did not, a default may only be entered against the second one. If neither responded, you would type in both of their names. On the third line, type in the title of your petition or complaint, such as *Complaint for Custody*.

3. Sign the form and fill in the date and your name, address, and telephone number on the appropriate lines. Take or send this form to the clerk, who will complete the bottom part of the form and return a copy to you. Once you receive the copy signed by the clerk, you may take or send an order to the judge for his or her signature.

If no hearing is necessary, once you receive the default signed by the clerk you can type the order you want the judge to sign following the instructions in this and other chapters, and send the original and four or five copies to the court for the judge to sign. You should include a self-addressed stamped envelope along with the order so that signed copies can be returned to you.

If a hearing is required, ask the clerk about the procedures for scheduling hearings on default judgments. Usually either the clerk or the judge's secretary handles the scheduling of hearings. In most cases, at the hearing the judge will grant your petition without requiring more than minimal evidence about why your requests should be granted.

Usually, your testimony alone will be sufficient for this purpose. If there is something unusual about your case, you can take other witnesses to the hearing or bring documents to show the judge. At the hearing, you should present a proposed order for the judge to sign.

Prepare your order following the instructions related to final orders (in a later section in this chapter) and adapting either form 13, form 14, form 18, or form 19 for your state. You will also need the last known mailing address for each of the parties, which you can provide to the court using form 29 (Certificate of Last Known Mailing Address). Once the judge has signed your order, your case is completed.

UNCONTESTED CASES

There are two basic ways litigation proceedings can go. If the parties are not able to reach an agreement as to what the outcome of the case will be, the case is contested and a judge or jury makes the final decision. In many cases, however, the parties are able to reach an agreement and the case is settled. Many factors influence the decision to settle a case, and many cases settle. In most cases, the parties are better off if they can settle. That way, you each have some control over the ultimate result instead of letting some stranger (the judge or jury) decide what happens with your grandchildren. Obviously, if you do settle, the legal procedures are much simpler.

AGREED ORDERS

If you reach an agreement with the other parties, you can finalize the agreement by preparing a final order setting out the terms of the agreement. Get each of the parties to sign the order before it is presented to the judge. You may or may not be required to schedule a hearing before the judge to get your order signed. The clerk of the court will be able to tell you what procedure you need to follow to get the order signed.

Provide several copies of the order to the court when you present it for signature. The clerk may keep two or three copies, and each of the parties will need a copy. One of the order forms in appendix C can be adapted as an order pursuant to an agreement, usually by changing the first paragraph to say something like: *Pursuant to the agreement of the parties as filed in this action, the court makes the following orders.*

AGREEMENT
(FORM 27)

You can use form 27 to spell out your agreement in either visitation or custody situations. Complete the case style portion according to the instructions in the section of chapter 3 or chapter 5 titled "Legal Forms." The title of this document will be either *Agreement Regarding Child Visitation*, or *Agreement Regarding Child Custody*. In the space below the introductory sentence, type in the details of your visitation or custody arrangement. At the end of the form are places for all parties to sign and fill in their names, addresses, and telephone numbers. Once this form is signed by all parties, it can be filed with the court clerk, along with an order for the judge to sign. The order must contain the same visitation or custody provisions as the Agreement.

CONTESTED CASES

Contested cases, of course, are much more complex. We have discussed the types of documents you will be filing to begin the lawsuit. Any time you file something with the court, you should keep a copy for your records. You should take or mail an extra copy when you file things so that you have a copy that bears the file stamp from the court. If you are intervening in an ongoing lawsuit or filing documents in a contested case, be sure you send a copy of whatever you file to all the other attorneys in the case by certified mail (or to the parties themselves if they do not have attorneys). If you are intervening, you will need to check the procedural rules for your state regarding service of process in interventions. Instead of sending copies by certified mail, you may need to serve the parties personally as described above. With all documents, except the original which you are probably having served by the sheriff, you will need to include a Certificate of Service at the end of the document or as a separate document (see form 7).

MOTIONS

As your case progresses, there may be things that you want the judge to do, such as. order a home study in a custody case. This is accomplished by filing a *motion* with the court. Generally, a motion is addressed to the judge and tells him or her what action you want taken and (briefly) why. Several motion forms are provided in appendix C and will be discussed individually later.

When you file your motion, you should also supply the clerk with a Notice of Hearing (form 10), which will be filled in following the clerk's instructions when your hearing is scheduled. A sample completed Notice of Hearing is included in appendix B as form L.

You will have to notify all the other parties or their attorneys of the time and place of the hearing. This should generally be done by certified mail. After the hearing, if the judge grants your request, you will need to supply an order for the judge to sign, along with several extra copies. The clerk will return the copies to you with the judge's signature or stamp on them. Keep a copy for yourself and send a copy to all the other parties or their attorneys.

MOTION AND ORDER FOR SOCIAL STUDY (FORM 20)

Form 20 can be used to ask the judge to have someone, usually a state agency, conduct a home study. (Usually this will only be done in custody cases, unless the parents make an issue of conditions in your home in a visitation case.) Someone from the agency will visit your home, and the home of the parents or anyone else seeking to get or keep custody, and will make a report to the judge of the suitability of each home. Complete the case style portion according to the instructions in the section of chapter 3 or chapter 5 titled "Legal Forms." Sign and date the form, and type in your name, address, and telephone number on the appropriate lines. Also complete a Certificate of Service (form 7), and mail a copy of your completed form 20 to all of the other parties. File the original of form 20 and form 7 with the court clerk. The judge will complete the bottom portion of the form, which will be the order.

MOTION AND ORDER FOR APPOINTMENT OF GUARDIAN AD LITEM (FORMS 21 AND 22)

Form 21 should be used if you want a guardian ad litem appointed for the child. A *guardian ad litem* is someone appointed by the court to independently and impartially represent the best interest of the child. (Usually this will only be done in custody cases.) Having an independent person support your contention that giving you custody would be in the child's best interest can help swing the case your way. Of course if the current custodian is just as suitable as you, you run a very real risk that the guardian ad litem will recommend that custody not be changed. Form 21 is self-explanatory, so just fill in the information required. Form 22 is an order you submit to the court along with your motion. All you need to do is fill in the information at the end of the form for who should receive copies. For both forms, be sure to complete the case style portion according to the instructions in the section of chapter 3 or chapter 5 titled "Legal Forms."

MOTION AND ORDER FOR PSYCHIATRIC/ PSYCHOLOGICAL EXAMINATION (FORMS 23 AND 24)

Form 23 should be used if you think a psychological evaluation would help show that you should have custody. (Usually this will only apply to custody cases, unless the parents make your psychological health an issue in a visitation case.) Check the lines for the items which apply in your situation, date and sign the form, and fill in the name, address, telephone number, and certificate of service. Then file form 23 along with form 24, which is the order for the judge to sign. For both forms, be sure to complete the case style portion according to the instructions in the section of chapter 3 or chapter 5 titled "Legal Forms."

MOTION TO PROCEED IN FORMA PAUPERIS (FORM 25)

If you are unable to pay for the court costs of filing, and the fee for personal service, you can file a Motion to Proceed In Forma Pauperis (form 25). This may be called by various names, depending upon the state. For example, in California it is called an *Application for Waiver of Court Fees and Costs*, and in Illinois it is called an *Application to Sue or Defend as a Poor Person*. Be aware that you will need to show a certain degree of poverty to qualify (you would probably have to be able to qualify for food stamps or other welfare benefits). Do not try this just because you would rather not pay the fees. Also, filing this form may not be a good idea if you are seeking custody. In a custody case, the question of your financial ability to care for the child will surely arise. On the other hand, with child support payments from the parents, you may still be better able to care for the child.

Form 25 can be used for this purpose, although be sure to check with the court clerk to see if there is an approved or required form for your court. Complete the case style portion according to the instructions in the section of chapter 3 or chapter 5 titled "Legal Forms." Fill in all of the financial information required in the form. Form 25 is in the form of an affidavit, so you will need to sign it before a notary public. File this form with the clerk. You will be notified if your motion is accepted, or if you will need to pay the filing and other fees.

DISCOVERY

In many states, you will have *discovery* devices available to you. Some of these are expensive; some are available at little or no cost. One inexpensive device is a set of interrogatories. *Interrogatories* are written questions that you send to another party. That party must then answer the questions. This is a way for you to learn who the witnesses are who will testify against you. You may also be able to send *requests for production of documents*. This is a series of categories of documents that you ask another party to supply to you, to either support your case or to learn more about their case against you. Another method of learning about the case against you is by taking a deposition. A *deposition* is when a witness testifies under oath before a certified shorthand reporter. This is a more expensive method because of the expense of the court reporter. Court reporter fees can typically run about $50 per hour for the reporter's time, and several dollars per page for typing up a transcript of the testimony. A one hour deposition can easily cost $200 in court reporter fees. If you are taking the deposition of an expert witness like a doctor or therapist, the witness will also have to be paid for his or her time. You will need to look up the procedural rules for your state to determine what the specific requirements are that govern these discovery devices and whether or not your state will allow you to use them in this type of a case.

WITNESSES
When it is time for your trial, you will need to notify your witnesses to be present. The safest way to do this is to get a subpoena and have it served on them. While you are not required to have a witness subpoenaed in order for them to testify, it is best to use a subpoena. Otherwise, the judge will probably not give you a continuance if something keeps your unsubpoenaed witnesses from appearing at the trial. A subpoena will also help your witnesses get time off from work to testify for you. If you intend to use an expert witness (like a doctor or police officer), you must use a subpoena. The subpoena is issued by the court clerk, and you should be able to get a form for requesting the subpoena from the clerk. Subpoena forms vary widely from state to state. Although there is a subpoena form included in the appendix, be sure to check the forms for your state. Your court clerk may be able to provide you with the subpoena form. If you want the witness to bring specific documents or other items, you will need to ask for a *subpoena duces tecum*. On the form requesting the subpoena duces tecum, you will need to list the documents or items you want the witness to bring, being as detailed and specific as necessary to leave no doubt about what is being requested.

SUBPOENA
(FORM 9)
Form 9 is a subpoena form, however, this may not be sufficient because most states have their own subpoena forms. Be sure to use the approved form for your court. Form 9 is designed to be used as either a subpoena to testify, or as a subpoena duces tecum (to bring documents or other things. An example of form 9, completed as a subpoena duces tecum, can be found as form K in appendix B. To complete:

1. Complete the case style portion according to the instructions in the section of chapter 3 or chapter 5 titled "Legal Forms."

2. After the word *to*, type in the name and address of the witness.

3. In the main body of the form, type in the judge's name, the address of the court and courtroom number (or whatever information is required to let the witness know exactly where he or she needs to go to testify), and the date and time of the hearing.

4. If you want this to be a subpoena duces tecum, type in the words *duces tecum* under the title *subpoena*. In the space after the first main paragraph, type in a description of the documents or other items you want the witness to bring to the hearing. Be as specific and detailed as possible, so there is no doubt what the person is being asked to bring. See form K in appendix B for an example.

5. Type in your name, address, and telephone number on the appropriate lines under the section entitled *Attorney or Party Requesting Subpoena*. This is so the witness can contact you if he or she has any questions.

6. Take the subpoena form to the court clerk, who will fill in the date and sign it. Once it is signed by the clerk, have the subpoena served on the witness by the sheriff or other authorized process server.

When the time for your trial arrives, you should be thoroughly prepared. Well in advance of the trial date, at least two months, you should have selected the witnesses who will testify for you and had them served with the subpoenas. You should have located all the documents you intend to use at the trial. Preparation for trial also means that you should know exactly what testimony you need from each witness and have written down the questions you need to ask. Try to be as concise as possible in questioning your witnesses. Do not ask about anything that is not relevant to the issues that the judge is going to be deciding. The judge will want to keep the trial moving and will not be happy if you waste time on unimportant matters.

Before the hearing, you will need to talk to each witness to be sure of what they will say in court. Never make assumptions about this—the surest way to lose your case is to have surprise testimony from a witness. In court, never ask a witness a question to which you do not already know the answer. Therefore, when you interview the witnesses, be sure to ask them every question you might be asking at the hearing. You should also ask the witness to tell you everything they know about your case. This will help you to not be surprised in court and you might learn something you did not know.

It is possible that a witness will tell you one thing in an interview and testify to something entirely different. One way to keep this from happening is to take the witness' deposition. If you decide this is too expensive, consider having the witness prepare a written signed statement. You can also take a third party with you to the interview to verify the statements made by the witness.

EXPERT
WITNESSES

In many cases, you will be using expert witnesses to testify in your behalf. A witness is an expert if their testimony is based on their special education, training, or experience—they are giving a professional opinion. At the hearing, you will need to ask these witnesses about their education and experience—this is called *qualifying the witness as an expert*. If you are using a doctor as an expert, you will need to talk to him or her several months before the hearing to determine whether they will come to court for you. Because of their busy schedules, most doctors prefer to testify by deposition, and they charge high hourly rates to come to court. The other parties will need to approve of using any such deposition for trial testimony. If you are in this situation, ask the doctor questions in the deposition just as though you were in court.

COURTROOM MANNERS

When you go to court, you should always be respectful. Remember, the judge will be making a decision that greatly impacts your relationship with your grandchildren. It is not a good idea to make the judge angry by being disrespectful, either to the judge or to another party. One of the ways you show respect is by the way you dress. You should always wear nice clothes to court, never shorts or sweat suits. Always stand up when the judge enters or leaves the courtroom and any time you talk to the judge. Always address the judge as "your Honor," no matter what you hear some of the attorneys in the courtroom say. Many attorneys address the judge as "judge," but this is incorrect. You should never argue with the judge or the other parties or their attorneys. When presenting your position or opposing a request by another party, speak to the judge, not to that party. It is important that you maintain control of your emotions. Displays of anger are never a good idea. Also, be sure you listen to the judge when he or she speaks and follow any instructions that you are given.

EVIDENTIARY RULES

The judge may give you instructions about what evidence you may or may not use. Before going to court, read the rules of evidence in civil cases for your state (there may be separate rules for criminal cases). These are important rules that you must follow in order to prove your case. For example, there are specific requirements for admitting documents into evidence. If you fail to follow the rules, you may not be able to use your documents.

HEARSAY

One major rule of evidence you are sure to encounter is the *hearsay rule*. Basically, *hearsay* is something someone told the witness who is testifying. As a general rule, witnesses cannot testify to something that someone else told them. For example, a friend cannot testify about something your grandchild's teacher told her; instead, the teacher must testify as a witness. Documents can also be excluded under the hearsay rule. For instance, a letter from your grandchild's teacher about your grandchild cannot be used in court because it is hearsay. There are, however, many exceptions to the hearsay rule and you need to familiarize yourself with them. Some things that would otherwise be excluded as hearsay (something the grandchild's mother told you is an example) can be used in court under the exception relating to admissions made by parties to the lawsuit. To avoid problems with this rule, try to be sure that your witnesses testify about what they know first-hand; not what they heard from someone else.

RELEVANCY

You will also encounter the *relevance* rule. Every document you use and every question you ask a witness must be relevant to the things you need to establish in order to win. For example, if your case is based on your grandchild being physically abused by the parent, testimony that the parent refused to let you talk to your grandchild on the telephone may not be relevant.

DOCUMENTS AND PHOTOGRAPHS

You will also run into specific rules about how to use documents and photographs. You will need to follow the rules for your state, but you will generally need to have a witness testify about the identity of the document or photo and the person who created the document or photo. A final tip on the rules of evidence—when questioning a witness, be sure to just ask questions without testifying yourself or making explanations.

TRIAL PROCEDURES

If you represent yourself, the judge may be helpful in guiding you through the trial procedures. If so, just follow his or her lead. Most trials follow the same format. Each party will first be given the chance to make a brief opening statement. The person who initiated the lawsuit (the plaintiff or petitioner) goes first. This is not the time to argue your case or cover all the facts. Just tell the judge what the issues are and what you want the final decision to be.

Once the opening statements are over, the trial begins and witnesses are called. The plaintiff or petitioner goes first again. They call a witness and ask their questions of that witness, then the other parties have an opportunity to cross-examine the witness. This process continues until the plaintiff has called all of his or her witnesses. Then the other parties call their witnesses. When all the parties have finished presenting their cases, the judge will allow each to make a final argument. In your final argument, review your most important points for the judge and ask him or her to do whatever it is you want done. After everyone has made an argument, the judge will announce the decision and tell the parties the outcome. The winning party will then be responsible for drafting the final judgment.

SAMPLE
OPENING
STATEMENT

Assume that you are a widowed paternal grandmother of two. The grandchildren's parents are divorced and the mother has custody. During the six years the parents were married, you saw your grandchildren regularly—in fact, they stayed with you every afternoon after school and at least one Saturday evening a month. However, in the year since the divorce, the mother has not allowed you to see the grandchildren. You, the mother, and the grandchildren all live in Wyoming. What follows is an opening statement which you might use in this situation:

> May it please the Court. My name is Jane Doe and I am the paternal grandmother of Sam and Sara Doe. I am here today seeking grandparent visitation pursuant to Section 20 - 7 - 101 (a)(i) of the Wyoming Statutes. Specifically, I intend to prove that after my son, Robert, and Wanda, the children's mother, divorced, Wanda got custody and has since refused me reasonable visitation with my grandchildren. Because I have had a close relationship with these children in the past, I believe my evidence will show that it is in their best interest to continue to see me on a regular basis. As I have had no success in getting to see my grandchildren any other way, I have come here today to ask you to order the mother, Wanda Doe, to allow me to see the grandchildren and to set a specific schedule for those visits. Thank you.

SAMPLE
CLOSING
STATEMENT

Using the same facts, here is a sample closing statement. For your case, you will want to add other significant facts from your hearing.

> May it please the Court. Your Honor, my grandchildren are very precious to me, and as you know from the evidence you have heard

today, I am very concerned about how the loss of our relationship has damaged them. Up until the time the children's parents divorced, I saw them every day after school and at least one weekend a month. I agree wholeheartedly with the psychologist, Dr. Dan Jones, when he says that maintaining this relationship is important to the emotional well-being of the children, especially during this vulnerable period after the divorce. I believe that the actions of the mother in keeping my grandchildren and me apart has harmed the children. This is verified by the change in their schoolwork—you can see from the report cards that their grades have been much worse since they quit staying with me after school. And the school counselor, Miss Smith, testified about how each of the children has talked to her about missing me and being hurt that their mother did not want them to see me. The mother has not put on any credible evidence to show why I should not see the kids because there is not any reason to keep me away from my grandchildren. The evidence has clearly shown that Wanda Doe has consistently refused reasonable visitation rights ever since she and my son divorced. Because of her actions, I qualify for visitation under Section 20 - 7 - 101 (a)(i) of the Wyoming Statutes. The evidence has overwhelmingly shown that visitation with me is in the children's best interest and that the rights of the parents are not substantially impaired if visitation is awarded. I, therefore, urge the Court to do the right thing for my grandchildren and order regular visitation, of at least once a month, for us. Thank you."

FINAL ORDER

Once the judge announces his or her decision, you will need to prepare a final order for the judge to sign. The actual title of this form is different in various states. It may be called a *Judgment, Decree, Final Order,* or something else. Generally, the final order should reflect the date of the hearing, the parties who were present, and the decision that the judge made. When you submit the final order to the judge to be signed, you should also send copies to the other parties. Before your final order is signed, the judge will give the other parties an opportunity to object to the form of the order. The judge may even require that all of the attorneys (or parties if they represent themselves) sign the judgment. This is not the time to object to the decision the judge made. The only appropriate objection is that the written judgment does not agree with the decision announced by the judge. Once the final order has been signed and everyone is sent a copy, the case is over unless there is an appeal.

Generally, the party who wins has the responsibility of preparing the final order. Appendix C contains four final order forms, two for visitation and two for custody. These may need to be modified to comply with the requirements of your particular state or court. (For examples of completed final orders, see form H and form M in appendix B.)

VISITATION
ORDER
(FORM 13)

Once the hearing is complete and the judge has awarded you visitation, your next hurdle is to insure that the order is properly drafted so that you can enforce your visitation rights if the parents still refuse to cooperate. It is important that the language in the order set the visitation schedule out very specifically and that the parents be ordered to surrender your grandchild to you for your periods of visitation. For example, if the judge has awarded you visitation on every fifth weekend of the month, the order should read like the one in form H in appendix B. Form 13 is for use in all states *except* Texas.

1. Complete the case style portion according to the instructions in the section of chapter 3 or chapter 5 titled "Legal Forms."

2. On the line in the first paragraph, type in the date of your court hearing.

3. In the *Visitation* paragraph, type your names on the first line, and your grandchildren's names on the second line. In the space after this paragraph, type in the visitation schedule ordered by the judge. Be as specific as possible as to such things as days and times, but don't add to (or subtract from) what the judge said.

Be sure to check the rules for your state to see if any other information (for example, the warnings on page 2 of the Texas example) is required.

DECREE GRANTING GRANDPARENT ACCESS (FORM 14)

Form 14 is the visitation order for use in Texas.

1. Complete the case style portion according to the instructions in the section of chapter 3 or chapter 5 titled "Legal Forms."

2. Fill in the date of your hearing in the first blank or leave it blank for the judge to complete.

3. Put your names in the second blank and the parents' names in the next blank, picking the option that applies. The first option is when the parent comes to court for the hearing, the second for when the parent files a waiver (see form 12).

4. In the findings section, list the names and statistical information for your grandchildren.

5. In the section marked *Orders*, state very *specifically* the visitation you are getting.

CHILD CUSTODY ORDER (FORM 18)

Form 18 is a custody order for use in all states *except* Texas. Some states have specific requirements for final judgments, so be sure to check the statutes for your state. For example, the Texas forms (see form 14 and form 19) have several paragraphs under the heading *Warnings to Parties*, which are required to be in all final decrees in Texas. For an example of form 18 completed, see form M in appendix B. To complete:

1. Complete the case style portion according to the instructions in the section of chapter 3 or chapter 5 titled "Legal Forms."

2. On the line in the first paragraph, type in the date of the final hearing.

3. On the line in the paragraph under the heading *Custody*, type in the name (or names) of who is to have custody. If all went well at the hearing, this will be your name (or your name and your spouse's name). In the space below this paragraph, type in the names of the children.

4. On the line in the paragraph under the heading *Visitation*, type in the name (or names) of the persons who will be receiving visitation rights. If all went well at the hearing, this will be the name of one or both of your grandchildren's parents. Even if you were not successful in obtaining custody at the hearing, you may be able to secure specific visitation rights which should be spelled-out in the final order. In the space below that paragraph, type in the details of the visitation ordered by the judge. Be as specific and detailed as possible, so that there is no doubt of exactly when visitation is to be allowed.

5. If child support has also been ordered, type in this information on the lines in the paragraph under the heading *Child Support*. On the first line, fill in the name of the person who was ordered to pay support. On the second and third lines fill in the amount of support and the period when each payment is owed (such as *week*, or *month*, etc.).

6. The paragraph under the heading *Costs*, is to designate who was ordered to pay the court costs.

7. Present the order to the judge for signing (either directly to the judge at the end of the hearing or to the judge's secretary later). Provide enough copies so one can be given or sent to each party.

DECREE FOR CHILD CUSTODY (FORM 19)

Form 19 is a custody order specifically for use in Texas. Form 19 is very similar to form 14, except that some additional matters relating to custody are included in form 19. To complete:

1. Complete the case style portion according to the instructions in the section of chapter 3 or chapter 5 titled "Legal Forms."

2. Follow the instructions on the previous page for Form 14 until you get to the heading titled *Conservatorship*.

3. Under the heading *Conservatorship*, type in the name (or names) of the person (or persons) who will have custody, and the names of the children.

4. Under the heading *Possession Order*, type in the name of the person (or persons) who will be receiving visitation, and the details of when visitation will be allowed.

5. The paragraph under the heading *Costs*, is to designate who was ordered to pay the court costs.

6. Present the order to the judge (either directly to the judge at the end of the hearing or to the judge's secretary later) for signing. Provide enough copies so that one can be given or sent to each party.

APPEALS

It is possible to appeal a decision made by the judge after a trial. The appeals process, which includes many strict deadlines, is not covered in this book and you will need to research this independently if it becomes an issue in your case.

The one thing you should know about appeals is that you can only appeal an issue of law; not an issue of fact. This means that if a judge finds that the facts of the case do not warrant visitation or custody, there is nothing to appeal. A party gets one day in court and an appeals court cannot substitute its judgment for that of the trial judge.

What can be appealed is if a judge makes an error in interpreting the law. For example, if a judge rules that a law is unconstitutional, or that it doesn't apply to certain parties when it actually does, you can have an appellate court rule on whether that is a correct interpretation of the law.

EVIDENCE YOU WILL NEED 8

VISITATION

Obviously, you will need much more extensive evidence in a custody case than in a visitation case. The first step in deciding what evidence you will need for your visitation case is to refer again to the eligibility requirements for your state. Let's say, for example, that you and your grandchild live in Wyoming and that the qualifying ground for visitation that you intend to use is that your grandchild has resided with you for seven months, then returned to live with the parents, and that you are not getting to see the grandchild. In that case, you will need evidence to prove that the grandchild resided with you for the seven months and that you are not getting visitation. Of course, you can testify to these facts as can other family members who know about either of these situations.

Other sources of proof include testimony from friends, neighbors, fellow church members, or members of clubs to which you belong. School and medical records are another good source of proof of your grandchild's residence. You will also need to show that visitation is in your grandchild's best interest. Photographs and videotapes showing you having fun with your grandchild are a good way to help establish the nature of your relationship. Other adults who have seen you interact with your grandchildren make good witnesses for this purpose. You may also want to have a psychologist or therapist testify about the importance of your grandchildren having a relationship with you.

CUSTODY

All of this same evidence will also be useful in custody cases. Once again, you will first need to look at the laws on custody for your state and tailor your evidence to that law. If child abuse or neglect is involved, you may be able to get evidence or testimony from public agencies like the Department of Human Services, Child Protective Services, (or whatever your state's child welfare department is called), the police department, or your grandchild's school. Most of these records are governed by confidentiality rules. If this is the case, you may need either a subpoena or court order to gain access to the records. If you need a court order, prepare a simple motion asking the court to order these records released to you. You can adapt one of the motion forms in the appendix (such as forms 20, 21, or 23). You will also need to prepare an order for the judge to sign. Look at form 22 or form 24 for an example of an order that goes with a motion. Babysitters and day care centers may be another source of evidence. If it is applicable to your case, remember to check with the appropriate alcohol or drug treatment center, family violence crises center, or rape crises center. Physicians and their records are also fertile ground for helpful evidence, as are any counselors or therapists that may have seen your grandchild, the parents, or the grandparents.

If your grandchildren are in a bad environment at home or exposed to unsavory characters while with their parents, you will need to locate people with personal knowledge of these facts to testify for you. Another item that may be helpful to you in a custody case is the *home study*. A home study results from the judge appointing a qualified, neutral third party to make an evaluation of all the parties involved in a case. This person then makes a recommendation to the judge as to who should get custody. If the facts of your case merit it, you can also ask the judge to order a psychological evaluation of the parties or drug testing. These evaluations by neutral third parties carry a great deal of weight with the judge and can be very helpful to you.

SPECIFIC CASE EXAMPLES 9

All of the material contained in this book is general in nature and must be adapted to fit the needs of your particular case. In order to give you some guidance, the following section contains some examples of specific, real-life cases. Where possible, the case citation is included. The citation is a set of numbers that tells you where to look up the case so that you can read the judge's opinion for yourself. The first number refers you to the volume of the set of books (called the *reporter*) that contains the case and the second number is the page number in the book. The number in parentheses is the year in which the case was decided by the court. The middle abbreviation tells you which set of reporters to use. The country is divided into regions and the regions each have their own reporters (see page 9 for more information on reporters). As a general rule, the following cases involve grandparents and have been appealed. It is generally the appeals court opinion to which the citations will direct you. First, an examination of visitation cases will be made.

VISITATION

An example of a worst-case scenario visitation case was discussed in the December 2, 1991, issue of *Newsweek*. In that case, the parents decided to restrict the grandparents to visiting with the children in the parents' home. The parties lived in Connecticut, which permits grandparent visitation if, in the court's best judgment, the visitation is in the best interest of the children. The grandparents decided to file for visitation, the parents contested, and the lawsuit became a mess. At the time of the *Newsweek* article, the case had been going on for almost two years and was still not resolved. It had mushroomed from one visitation lawsuit into five different lawsuits and thousands of dollars in legal fees.

Other contested cases are less difficult. In the case of *Rosemary E.R. v. Michael G.Q.*, 471 A.2d 995 (1984), the maternal grandmother sought visitation with her six-year-old grandchild. The grandmother, who was eighty years old, confined to a wheelchair, and lived with her seventy-five-year-old sister, was found by the court as suitable for visitation and as having a happy relationship with her other grandchildren. Her daughter (the child's mother) was dead and the father had remarried. The father opposed the visits because the child had adjusted well to the new family situation and because the grandmother might not be able to supervise the child. The judge denied the visitation, saying the grandmother had not proved that visitation was in the child's best interest.

In the case of *Ehrlich v. Ressner*, 391 N.Y.S. 152 (1977), the grandparents sought visitation with their teenage grandchildren. In this case, the judge gave the grandparents visitation even though the grandchildren testified that they did not want to have to visit with their grandparents.

In another New York case, *Emmanuel S. v. Joseph E.*, 577 N.E.2d 27 (1991), the paternal grandparents sought visitation because their relationship with the parents had deteriorated when the grandchild was about three months old and they no longer saw the grandchild. The judge gave these grandparents six hours of visitation on the second Sunday of every month.

In a third New York case, *Seymour S. v. Glen S.*, 592 N.Y.S. 411 (1993), the paternal grandfather sued for visits over the parents' objections. The court did not give this grandparent visitation because he had not made reasonable efforts to establish contact with the grandchild before he filed suit, had alienated both of his own sons, and had not had any contact with the child's father for two years.

Other New York cases illustrate the problems grandparents can face, even though they meet the technical requirements of the visitation statute. In *Matter of Coulter v. Barber*, 632 N.Y.S.2d 270 (1995), and other cases, courts have held that grandparent visitation is not generally permitted over the objections of both parents.

In Pennsylvania, in a case called *Suroviec v. Mitchell*, 500 A.2d 894 (1985), the grandparents, who were the parents of the children's deceased mother, had cared for the grandchildren for three years when the parents and grandchildren lived with the grandparents. After the mother's death, the father remarried and refused visitation. After hearing testimony from the parties, including the grandchildren and expert psychological testimony, the judge gave the grandparents five hours of visitation per month.

Sometimes you may read cases from your state that seem to directly contradict each other. For example, compare the following cases from Illinois: *In Re Marriage of Lindsay*, 511 N.E.2d 198 (1987), says that normally loving, caring, and reasonable grandparents should be allowed unrestricted visitation. But *In Re Marriage of Balzell*, 566 N.E.2d 20 (1991), says that special circumstances must exist in order to justify grandparent visitation. If you find yourself in this situation, you will need to do some additional research to determine which case more closely applies to your situation. It may be that the more recent case will govern. It may also be that some cases reached a different result because of the particular facts of that case and are only applied in narrowly defined circumstances. Finally, it may also be that the judge simply didn't like either the parents or the grandparents, and found a way to justify the decision he or she made (of course, you often won't be able to know this from reading the case). Try to find the most recent case whose facts most closely resemble yours. It may also help to look for trends, such as how many cases came out one way or the other.

Another example of a visitation case is *Drennen v. Drennen*, 557 N.E.2d 149 (1988), in which the paternal grandparents sought visitation, but the court refused to grant it because the grandparents had allowed their son, who had been convicted of attempting to rape the mother in front of the child, to be alone with the child. The court used this fact to defeat the best interest claim of the grandparents.

Finally, the highest courts in Florida, Tennessee, and Washington have declared those states' grandparent visitation statutes unconstitutional. These cases may signal a trend that will spread to other states, so you should make sure of the status of the law in your state before you file for visitation. Be sure to see "Recent Developments" on page 13 for a more detailed discussion of these cases.

CUSTODY

For illustration purposes, a few sample custody cases follow. In Alaska, the paternal grandparents filed for custody in *Bass v. Bass*, 437 P.2d 324(1968). The court gave custody to the grandparents because they proved that the mother was emotionally immature, generally neglected the child's physical needs, and did not pay much attention to the health of the child.

Another case in which grandparents got custody is from North Dakota, *Mansukhami v. Pailing*, 318 N.W.2d 748 (1982). In that case, the paternal grandparents had cared for the grandchildren. Their son was deceased and had not provided support or care for the children while alive. During the separation, divorce, and reconciliation between the parents, the grandchildren lived with the grandparents while the parents lived in another town. The mother later remarried and wanted custody. The grandparents got custody because all of the expert witnesses who testified said that giving custody to the mother would be detrimental to the children and because the judge felt that the grandchildren saw the grandparents as their "psychological parents."

Another case, although it did not involve grandparents, shows how the parental preference can defeat a grandparent's claim for custody. In that case, the nonparent did not get custody even though the parents had left the child with the nonparent for three years. During that time, the parents did not provide support or have contact with the child. When the father later sued for custody, he won because parents have preference over nonparents. Grandparents will encounter similar problems in states with the parental preference.

If you want to read other cases, there will be a list of cases following the statutes relating to grandparent visitation and to custody. It would be a good idea for you to read some of the cases from your state to get an idea of how the judges interpret the laws and of what evidence has been successful. As you can see from the above examples, cases do not always come out the way you think they will or even the way you think they ought to come out.

If you are confused, and it seems that some of these cases contradict each other, you are beginning to understand the confusing and unpredictable legal system with which you are about to deal.

Conclusion

Being a grandparent can be a rich and rewarding experience. It is always sad when family relationships become so strained that you end up in the court system. But if you do, this book has given you the basic tools to help you either represent yourself or work more effectively with an attorney.

Appendix A
State Laws

The following section contains a state-by-state listing of the applicable laws relating to grandparent visitation and custody. While every effort has been made to provide up-to-date information, the law can change at any time. Therefore, it is important for you to consult the current laws for your state to be sure you satisfy all of the legal requirements. Refer back to the section on "Legal Research" in chapter 1 for more information about researching the law for your state.

Warning

A trend of courts declaring grandparent visitation statutes unconstitutional may be beginning. See the subsection on "Recent Developments" on page 13 for a discussion of these cases. As this book goes to press, such statutes in Florida, Tennessee, and Washington have been declared unconstitutional. However, it is very possible that other states will do the same, so you are advised to check for recent court decisions in your state before filing for visitation. None of these decisions affect custody cases.

Explanation of Terms

The following is an explanation of what information may be found under each of the headings in this appendix:

The law: The first listing you will find is titled "The Law." This directs you to the title of the book where the laws for that state may be found. An abbreviation for the law, which is used in the following sections, is also given. The symbol "§" means "section." For some states, information is also given to try to help you find the specific volume or volumes you will need. For example, a direction to "ignore volume numbers" means that the books will give both a volume number and a section or chapter number on the cover. Use the section or chapter number, not the volume number. If the section number is followed by "et seq." it means that the reference begins there and continues in several following sections in sequence.

Grandparent visitation: This listing tells you the various grounds you may use to get grandparent visitation. These are the grounds that should be stated in your complaint or petition for visitation. The statutory provision relating to grandparent visitation is also given. Other information may also be given, such as whether other documents are required.

Effect of adoption: The section on effect of adoption tells you whether or not you can still have visitation rights with your grandchild if your child's parental rights have been terminated and the grandchild is adopted by someone else, either a stepparent or a stranger.

Custody statutes: This section tells you where to look for the general laws pertaining to child custody for your state, and gives a summary of what factors are considered. The factors are those used in divorces cases; however, they will also give you an idea of what criteria may be used in your case for grandparent custody.

Parental preference: This section tells you whether or not your state has a parental preference. Remember, the strength of the preference varies from state to state and you will need to read some of the annotations for your state to determine how strong this preference is.

ALABAMA

The law: Code of Alabama Title 30. "C.A." Ignore volume numbers.

Grandparent visitation: Divorce pending, one parent is deceased and surviving parent denies reasonable visitation, or grandparent unreasonably denied visitation for period exceeding 90 days. Title 30, Chapter 3 (C.A. §30-3-4 et seq.).

Effect of adoption: Natural grandparents may have post-adoption visitation when the child is adopted by a stepparent, another grandparent, brother, sister, half-brother or sister, an aunt or uncle and their respective spouses.

Custody statutes: Factors: (1) moral character of parents; and (2) age and sex of child. C.A., §30-3.

Parental preference: Yes.

ALASKA

The law: Alaska Statutes. "A.S." Ignore volume numbers; look for "title" numbers. Supplement is in the front of each volume.

Grandparent visitation: Grandparents may be awarded visitation in an action for divorce, legal separation, or for placement of the child; or when both parents have died; if it is in the best interest of the child. Title 25, Section 25.24.150 (A.S. §25.24.150)

Effect of adoption: Adoption terminates any rights unless the adoption decree specifically provides for visitation between the adopted child and the natural relatives.

Custody: Best interest of the child considering: (1) physical, emotional, mental, religious, and social needs of the child; (2) capability and desire of each party to meet those needs; (3) child's preference; (4) love and affection existing between child and each party; (5) length of time the child has been in a stable, satisfactory environment, and the desirability of maintaining continuity; (6) desire and ability of each party to allow an open and loving frequent relationship between the child and other party; (7) any evidence of domestic violence, child abuse or neglect, or history of violence between the parties; (8) any evidence of substance abuse by a party or other household member that directly affects the child; or (9) any other relevant factor. A.S. §25.24.150.

Parental preference: Yes.

ARIZONA

The law: Arizona Revised Statutes Annotated. "A.R.S." Ignore volume numbers; look for "section" numbers.

Grandparent visitation: Either parents' marriage dissolved for at least three months, parent of the child is deceased or missing for at least three months and parent reported missing, or child born out of wedlock. A.R.S. §25-409.

Effect of adoption: Visitation rights automatically terminate upon placement for adoption unless the adoption is by a stepparent.

Custody: Best interest of child considering: (1) parties' wishes; (2) child's wishes; (3) interaction and interrelationship between the child and each parent, siblings and other significant persons; (4) child's adjustment to home, school and community; (5) mental and physical health of all persons involved; (6) which parent is more likely to allow frequent and continuing contact with the other parent; (7) if one parent, both parents, or neither parent has provided primary care of the child; (8) the nature and extent of coercion or duress used by a parent in obtaining an agreement regarding custody; and (9) whether a parent has complied with Chapter 3, Article 5 (the domestic relations education section). A.R.S. §§ 25-401 to 25-414.

Parental preference: Yes.

ARKANSAS

The law: Arkansas Code of 1987 Annotated. "A.C.A." Look for "title" or "chapter" numbers.

Grandparent visitation: Grand parents may seek visitation order: (1) if the parents' marriage is terminated by death, divorce, or legal separation; (2) if the child is in the custody or guardianship of a person other than one or both of his natural or adoptive parents; or (3) if the child is born out-of-wedlock (for paternal grandparents to qualify, paternity must have been legally established). In all cases, the court must determine visitation is in the best interest of the child. Title 9, Chapter 13, Section 9-13-103 (A.C.A. §9-13-103).

Effect of adoption: Adoption terminates all rights of grandparents.

Custody: Only statutory provision is that custody is to be determined "without regard to the sex of the parent but solely in accordance with the welfare and best interests of the children." A.C.A. §9-13-101 et seq.

Parental preference: Yes.

CALIFORNIA

The law: Deering's California Codes Annotated, Family Code. Be sure you use the volume marked "Family." [There is also a set called "West's Annotated California Codes," which will contain the same section numbers.]

Grandparent visitation: If parent deceased, parents and grandparents of the deceased parent get visitation if in child's best interest. Otherwise, parents must be divorced or currently living separately and apart on a permanent or indefinite basis, one parent absent for over a month and the other parent does not know that parent's whereabouts, one parent must join in the petition with the grandparents, or the child must not be residing with either parent. Court must also find that there is a preexisting relationship between the grandparents and the grandchild such that visitation is in the child's best interest, and the court must balance the interest of the child in having visitation with the parents' right to exercise their parental authority. There is a rebuttable presumption that visitation is not in the best interest of the child if both parents agree that the grandparent should not be granted visitation. Family Code, Section 3100 et seq. (Family Code §3100 et seq.).

Effect of adoption: Natural grandparents may still get visitation.

Custody statutes: Factors: (1) child's preference (if child is old enough); (2) desire and ability of each parent to allow relationship with other parent, and (3) child's health, safety and welfare. Family Code § 3020-3424.

Parental preference: Yes.

COLORADO

The law: West's Colorado Revised Statutes Annotated. "C.R.S.A."

Grandparent visitation: Parents' marriage has been declared invalid or dissolved, or court order of legal separation entered, legal custody of the child given to a third party or child placed outside home of either parent (except for children who have been adopted or placed for adoption), or the grandparent must be the parent of the child's parent who has died. Title 19, Article 1, Section 19-1-117 (C.R.S.A. §19-1-117 et seq.). Additional affidavit required.

Effect of Adoption: Grandparent visitation rights automatically terminate upon completion of adoption by anyone other than a stepparent.

Custody statutes: Best interest of the child considering: (1) parties' wishes; (2) child's wishes; (3) interaction and interrelationship between child and parties, siblings and other significant persons; (4) child's adjustment to home, school and community; (5) mental and physical health of all persons involved; (6) custodian's ability to encourage sharing, love, affection and contact with the other party; (7) evidence of parties ability to cooperate and make joint decisions; (8) evidence of each party's ability to encourage sharing, love, affection and contact with other party; (9) any history of abuse or neglect, (10) any history of spouse abuse; and (11) various other factors relating to joint custody. C.R.S.A. § 14-10-123 et seq.

Parental preference: No.

CONNECTICUT

The law: Connecticut General Statutes Annotated. "C.G.S.A." Ignore "chapter" numbers; look for "title" numbers.

Grandparent visitation: Upon the court's best judgment of facts of the case and the best interest of the child and subject to the conditions and limitations the court deems equitable. Title 46b, Section 46b-59 (C.G.S.A. §46b-59).

Effect of adoption: Grandparents may still get visitation after their natural grandchild is adopted.

Custody statutes: Best interest of child considering (1) wishes of the child, if of sufficient age; and (2) causes of the parents' divorce as they may be relevant to the child's best interest. C.G.S.A. §46b-56.

Parental preference: No.

DELAWARE

The law: Delaware Code Annotated. "D.C.A." Ignore volume numbers; look for "title" numbers.

Grandparent visitation: Best interest of the child. Title 13, Section 728 (13 D.C.A. §728).

Effect of adoption: Adoption terminates all rights.

Custody statutes: Best interests of the child considering: (1) wishes of the parents and the child, (2) interaction and interrelationship of child with parents, siblings, and other significant persons; (3) child's adjustment to home, school and community; (4) mental and physical health of all persons involved. D.C.A. 13 §721. Must submit affidavit that Petitioner has been advised of the following children's rights: "(1) the right to a continuing relationship with both parents; (2) the right to be treated as an important human being, with unique feelings, ideas, and desires; (3) the right to continuing care and guidance from both parents; (4) the right to know and appreciate what is good in each parent without one parent degrading the other; (5) the right to express love, affection, and respect for each parent without having to stifle that love because of disapproval by the other parent; (6) the right to know that the parents' decision to divorce was not the responsibility of the child; (7) the right not to be a source of argument between the parents; (8) the right to honest answers to questions about the changing family relationships; (9) the right to be able to experience regular and consistent contact with both parents and the right to know the reason for any cancellation of time or change of plans; and (10) the right to have a relaxed, secure relationship with both parents without being placed in a position to manipulate one parent against the other." See 13 D.C.A. §701 and13 D.C.A. §721 et seq.

Parental preference: Yes.

District of Columbia

The law: District of Columbia Code. "D.C.C."

Grandparent visitation: No statutory provisions for grandparent visitation.

Custody statutes: No mention of grandparents, but following criteria are used in divorce cases: Best interest of the child considering: (1) wishes of the child; (2) wishes of the parties; (3) interaction and interrelationship between the child and parents, siblings and other significant persons; (4) child's adjustment to home, school and community, and (5) mental and physical health of all persons involved. District of Columbia Code, Title 16, Sections 911 & 914 (D.C.C. §§ 16-911 & 16-914).

Florida

The law: Florida Statutes. "F.S." A new set is published every odd-numbered year, with hard-cover supplements every even-numbered year. Ignore volume numbers; look for "chapter" numbers. [There is also a set called "West's Florida Statutes Annotated," which includes supplements in the back of each volume.]

Grandparent visitation: [*Special Note:* The Florida Supreme Court has declared the Florida grandparent visitation statute unconstitutional. For more information, see "Recent Developments" on page 13.] The statute provides for grandparent visitation if (1) at least one of the child's parents is deceased; or (2) the marriage of the child's parents is dissolved; or (3) a parent of the child has deserted the child; or (4) a child is born out of wedlock and not later determined to be a child born in wedlock; or (5) if the child is living with both parents who are still married to each other, whether or not there is a broken relationship between either or both parents and the grandparents, and either or both parents have used their parental authority to prohibit a relationship between the child and the grandparent. For all grounds, the court must determine that visitation is in the best interest of the child, and the court must consider the following factors: (1) the willingness of the grandparent to encourage a close relationship between the child and the parents; (2) the length and quality of the prior relationship between the child and the grandparent; (3) the preference of the child if the child is or sufficient maturity to express a meaningful preference; (4) the mental and physical health of the child; (5) the mental and physical health of the grandparent; and (6) any other factor necessary in the particular circumstances. Must also file UCCJA Affidavit. Chapter 752, Section 752.01 (F.S §752.01 et seq.).

Effect of adoption: Rights terminate unless the adoption is by a stepparent.

Custody statutes: Best interest of child considering: (1) which party is more likely to allow frequent and continuing contact with the other party; (2) love, affection and other emotional ties existing between the child and each party; (3) each party's capacity and disposition to provide food, clothing, medical care or other material needs for the child; (4) length of time the child has been in a stable, satisfactory environment, and the desirability of maintaining continuity; (5) the permanence, as a family unit, of the existing or proposed custodial home; (6) moral fitness of the parties; (7) mental and physical health of the parties; (8) child's home, school and community record; (9) preference of the child, if of sufficient intelligence, understanding and experience; and (10) any other relevant factor. F.S. §61.13(3).

Parental preference: Yes.

GEORGIA

The law: Official Code of Georgia Annotated. "C.G.A." Ignore volume numbers; look for "title" and "chapter" numbers. [This is not the same set as the "Georgia Code," which is a separate set of books with a completely different numbering system. If all you can find is the Georgia Code, look for a cross-reference table to the Official Code of Georgia.]

Grandparent visitation: Grandparent may intervene in any action in which a question concerning custody of minor child, divorce of parents, termination of the parental rights, or visitation rights is before the court, or whenever there has been an adoption by the child's blood relative or a stepparent. Title 19, Chapter 9, Section 3 (C.G.A. §19-9-3).

Effect of adoption: Rights do not terminate as long as the adoption is by a blood relative of the child or by the child's stepparent.

Custody statutes: No specific factors. Child may choose if at least 14 years of age, unless parent determined to be unfit. C.G.A. §19-9 et seq.

Parental preference: Yes.

HAWAII

The law: Hawaii Revised Statutes. "H.R.S." Ignore volume numbers; look for "title" numbers.

Grandparent visitation: Grandparent may seek visitation if: (1) Hawaii is the home state of the child at the time of commencement of the proceedings; and (2) visitation is in the best interest of the child; and (3) either both parents are deceased, or the parents are divorced or residing separate and apart. Title 574, Section 574-46.3 (H.R.S. §574-46.3).

Effect of adoption: Adoption terminates all rights.

Custody statutes: Best interest of child considering: (1) child's wishes, if of sufficient age and capacity to reason; and (2) any evidence of family violence. H.R.S. §583-1 et seq.

Parental preference: No.

IDAHO

The law: Idaho Code. "I.C." Ignore volume number.

Grandparent visitation: Visitation may be granted upon a showing that the visitation would be in the best interest of the child. [*Note:* If the grandparent's child who is the parent is also a minor, the grandparent can be ordered to pay child support for the grandchild until the parent is 18 years of age.] Title 32, Section 32-719 (I.C. §32-719).

Effect of adoption: Adoption terminates all rights.

Custody statutes: Best interest of child considering: (1) wishes of parties; (2) wishes of child; (3) interaction and interrelationship between the child and parties, siblings and other significant persons; (4) adjustment to home, school and community; (5) mental and physical health of all persons involved; (6) need to promote continuity and stability in the child's life; and (7) any history of domestic violence. I.C. §32-717.

Parental preference: Yes.

ILLINOIS

The law: West's Smith Hurd Illinois Compiled Statutes Annotated. "I.C.S." [This is not "Smith-Hurd Illinois Annotated Statutes," which is a separate set of books with a different numbering system.]

Grandparent visitation: Visitation may be granted if (1) the parents are not cohabiting on a permanent or indefinite basis; (2) one of the parents has been absent from the martial residence for over one month without the other spouse knowing his/her whereabouts; (3) one of the parents is deceased; (4) one of the parents joins in the petition with the grandparents or great-grandparents; or (5) a sibling is in state custody. Grandparents may not get visitation (1) if they are the paternal grandparents of a child born out-of-wedlock and for whom paternity has not been legally established; or (2) if the child is voluntarily surrendered by the parents to anyone other than the Illinois Department of Children and Family Services or a foster care facility. Title 750 Illinois Compiled Statutes, Section 5/607 (750 I.C.S. §5/607).

Effect of adoption: Visitation rights terminate unless the adoption is by a stepparent.

Custody statutes: Best interest of child considering: (1) wishes of parents and child; (2) interaction and interrelationship between the child and parents, siblings and other significant persons; (3) adjustment to home, school and community; (4) mental and physical health of parties and child; (5) any physical threat to child; (6) each party's willingness to encourage and facilitate continued contact between the other parent and the child. 750 I.C.S. §5/602 et seq.

Parental preference: Yes.

INDIANA

The law: West's Annotated Indiana Code. "A.I.C." Look for "title" numbers.

Grandparent visitation: Visitation may be granted if either the child's parent is deceased; the parents' marriage has been dissolved in Indiana; or if the child was born out of wedlock. (For the paternal grandparents of a child born out of wedlock to obtain visitation, the child's father must have legally established paternity.) If the marriage of the parents was dissolved somewhere other than Indiana, the grandparents may seek visitation if the custody decree does not bind the grandparent under I.C. §31-1-11.6-12 and if an Indiana court has jurisdiction under I.C. §31-1-11.6-14. In all cases, the court must determine that visitation is in the child's best interest, considering whether the grandparent has had, or attempted to have, meaningful contact with the child. Title 31, Article 1, Chapter 11.7, Section 1 (A.I.C. §31-1-11.7-1 et seq.).

Effect of adoption: Visitation rights terminate unless the adoption is by the child's stepparent or by a person who is biologically related to the child as a grandparent, sibling, aunt, uncle, niece, or nephew.

Custody statutes: Best interest of child considering: (1) age and sex of child; (2) wishes of parents and child; (3) interaction and interrelationship between the child and parents, siblings and other significant persons; (4) child's adjustment to home, school and community; and (5) mental and physical health of all persons involved. A.I.C. §31-1-11 et seq.

Parental preference: Yes.

IOWA

The law: Iowa Code Annotated. "I.C.A." Ignore volume numbers; look for "section" numbers.

Grandparent visitation: Visitation may be awarded if (1) either the child's parents are divorced; (2) a petition for dissolution of the marriage is pending; (3) the parent who is the child of the petitioning grandparents is deceased; (4) the child has been placed in a foster home; (5) the petitioning grandparents are the parents of the non-custodial parent and the other parent's spouse has adopted the child; or (6) the grandparent is the parent of the child's non-custodial parent and the child had been born out of wedlock. Visitation may also be permitted if a parent of the child unreasonably refuses to allow visitation or unreasonably restricts visitation (this applies, but is not limited to, situations where the parents are divorced and the parent who is that grandparent's child has custody). The court must also determine that visitation is in the child's best interest, and that the grandparent has established a substantial relationship with the child. Also, visitation can be ordered by the juvenile court as a part of a dispositional or permanency hearing, or in a guardianship proceedings. Iowa Code Annotated, Section 598.35 (I.C.A. §598.35).

Effect of adoption: Visitation rights terminate unless the adoption is by a stepparent.

Custody statutes: Best interest of child "which will assure the child the opportunity for the maximum continuing physical and emotional contact with both parents." I.C.A. §598.21.

Parental preference: Yes.

KANSAS

The law: Kansas Statutes Annotated. "K.S.A." You may find these either as "Vernon's Kansas Statutes Annotated," or "Kansas Statutes Annotated, Official." Both sets have very poor indexing systems.

Grandparent visitation: Visitation may be granted in a custody order. Kansas Statutes Annotated, Section 60-1616 (K.S.A. §60-1616).

Effect of adoption: Adoption terminates rights unless you are the parent of the child's deceased parent and the surviving parent's spouse adopts.

Custody statutes: Best interest of child considering: (1) any agreement of the parties; (2) length of time child has been under actual care and control of any person other than a parent and the circumstances involved; (3) desires of the parties; (4) desires of child; (5) interaction and interrelationship between child and parties, siblings and other significant persons; (6) child's adjustment to home, school and community; (7) each party's willingness and ability to respect and appreciate the bond between the child and the other party; (8) any evidence of spousal abuse; and (9) any other relevant factor. K.S.A. §60-16-1610(a)(3). Four types of custody are recognized, in the following order of preference: (1) joint; (2) sole; (3) divided (if 2 or more children); and (4) non-parental. K.S.A. §60-1610(a)(3).

Parental preference: Yes.

KENTUCKY

The law: Kentucky Revised Statutes. "KRS." Ignore volume numbers; look for "chapter" numbers. These are in a binder, with updates found in the beginning of each volume in a section marked "Current Service."

Grandparent visitation: Visitation may be granted if the court determines that the visitation is in the best interest of the child. A grandparent can get the same visitation as that awarded to a non-custodial parent, if that grandparent's child is deceased and the grandparent has assumed the financial obligation of child support, unless the court finds that this would not be in the child's best interest. Chapter 405, Section 021 (KRS §405.021).

Effect of adoption: Visitation rights terminate except in the case of a stepparent adoption where there has been no termination of the parental rights of the parent whose parents are seeking visitation. Once a grandparent has been granted visitation rights, those rights will not be adversely affected by the termination of parental rights of that grandparent's child, unless the court determines that it is in the child's best interest to do so.

Custody statutes: Best interest of child considering: (1) wishes of parents and child; (2) interaction and interrelationship between child and parents, siblings and other significant persons; (3) child's adjustment to home, school and community; and (4) mental and physical condition of all persons involved. KRS §405.020 et seq. and §403 et seq.

Parental preference: Yes.

Louisiana

The law: Louisiana Statutes Annotated-Revised Statutes ("LSA-R.S."), Children's Code ("Ch. C"), and Civil Code ("CC"). The books containing the laws of Louisiana are one of the more complicated sets of any state. There are several sets of books divided into subjects. All sets have the title of either "Louisiana Statutes Annotated," or "West's LSA," which is followed by the area of law such as Revised Statutes, Civil Code, Civil Procedure, etc. The divorce laws were completely rewritten in 1990, and may be found in a separate soft-cover volume titled "West's Louisiana Statutes Annotated, Civil Code." Look for a subheading titled "Ch.1. The Divorce Action."

Grandparent visitation: Visitation may be granted to the parents of a deceased parent or parent who has been declared legally incompetent if it is found to be in the best interest of the child. Louisiana Statutes Annotated-Revised Statutes, Article 9:344 (LSA-R.S. 9:344), and Children's Code, Article 1264 (Ch. C Art. 1264).

Effect of adoption: The natural parents of a deceased party to a marriage dissolved by death and the parents of a party who has forfeited his right to object to the adoption of his child pursuant to Article 1245 of the Children's Code may have limited visitation rights to a minor child who has been adopted.

Custody statutes: Joint legal custody is preferred and presumed best for the child. Parties must submit a joint custody plan. A party requesting sole custody must prove it is in the child's best interest considering the following factors: (1) the child's love, affection and emotional ties with each parent; (2) capacity and disposition of the parties to give love, affection, guidance, education, and religious guidance; (3) capacity and disposition of the parties to give the child food, clothing, medical care, etc., (4) length of time the child has been in a stable, satisfactory environment, and the desirability for continuity; (5) permanence as a family unit of the existing or proposed home; (6) moral fitness of the parties; (7) mental and physical health of the parties; (8) home, school and community record of the child; (9) preference of the child, if old enough; (10) willingness of each party to facilitate a relationship between the child and the other spouse; (11) distance between parties residences; and (12) any other factor the judge decides is proper (except race). LSA-C.C., Art. 131 et seq.

Parental preference: Yes.

MAINE

The law: Maine Revised Statutes Annotated. "M.R.S.A." Ignore volume numbers; look for "title" numbers.

Grandparent visitation: Visitation may be granted if at least one of the child's parents or legal guardians has died. In all cases, the visitation must be in the child's best interest and not significantly interfere with any parent-child relationship. In determining the child's best interest, the court must consider: (1) the child's age; (2) the relationship of the child with the grandparent, including the amount of previous contact; (3) the preference of the child, if old enough to express a meaningful choice; (4) the duration and adequacy of the child's current living arrangement, and the desirability of maintaining continuity; (5) the stability of the proposed living arrangement; (6) the motivation of the parties and their capacity to give love, affection, and guidance; (7) the child's adjustment to home, school, and community; (8) the capacity of parent and grandparent to cooperate or learn to cooperate in child care; (9) the methods of assisting cooperation and resolving disputes and each person's willingness to learn those methods; and (10) any other factor having a reasonable bearing on the physical and psychological well-being of the child. Title 19, Maine Revised Statutes Annotated, Section 1801 (19 M.R.S.A. §1801 et seq.). Additional affidavit required.

Effect of adoption: Adoption terminates all rights.

Custody statutes: Best interest of child considering: (1) child's age, (2) child's relationship with each party and other significant persons; (3) preference of child, if of suitable age and maturity; (4) duration and adequacy of child's current living arrangement, and desirability of maintaining continuity; (5) stability of proposed living arrangement; (6) motivation of the parties and their capacity to give love, affection and guidance; (7) child's adjustment to home, school and community; (8) each party's capacity to allow and encourage a relationship between the child and the other party; (9) each party's capacity to cooperate in child care; (10) the methods for assisting parental cooperation and resolving disputes, and each party's willingness to use those methods; (11) effect on the child if one party has sole authority regarding upbringing; (12) any history of domestic abuse; and (13) any other relevant factor. 19 M.R.S.A. §§ 214 & 752.

Parental preference: Yes.

MARYLAND

The law: Annotated Code of Maryland- Family Law. "A.C.M." Be sure you have the volume marked "Family Law."

Grandparent visitation: An equity court may grant a grandparent's request for reasonable visitation if it is found to be in the child's best interest. Case law sets out the factors to be considered in determining the best interests: (1) the nature and stability of the child's relationship with the parents; (2) the nature and stability of the relationship between the child and the grandparent, taking into account the frequency or contact, regularity of contact, and amount of time spent together; (3) the potential benefits and detriments to the child; (4) the effect visits would have on the child's attachment to the nuclear family; (5) the physical and emotional health of the adults involved; and (6) the stability of the child's living and schooling arrangements. Article 9, Section 9-102 (A.C.M. Family Law §9-102).

Effect of adoption: All rights terminate upon adoption.

Custody statutes: No statutory factors. Custody discussed at A.C.M. Family Law §9-101 et seq.

Parental preference: Yes.

MASSACHUSETTS

The law: Annotated Laws of Massachusetts. "A.L.M."

Grandparent visitation: Visitation may be granted if the child's parents are divorced, married but living apart under a temporary order or judgment of separate support, one of the parents is deceased, or if the child was born out of wedlock and paternity established by a court or by acknowledgment by the father and the child's parents live apart, if the visitation is in the child's best interest. Chapter 119, Section 39D (A.L.M. Chapter 119 §39D). Must include "care and custody affidavit" with petition.

Effect of adoption: Rights terminate upon adoption by anyone other than a stepparent.

Custody statutes: No specific factors in statute; only general concepts. A.L.M., Chapter 208 §31.

Parental preference: Yes.

MICHIGAN

The law: Michigan Statutes Annotated ("M.S.A."), or Michigan Compiled Laws Annotated ("M.C.L.A."). Michigan has two separate sets of laws, each by a different publisher. Each set has a cross-reference index to the other set. Ignore volume and "chapter" numbers; look for "section" numbers.

Grandparent visitation: Visitation can only be granted when the parents' marriage is declared invalid or dissolved or the court enters a decree of legal separation or legal custody of the child is given to a party other than the child's parent. Michigan Statutes Annotated, Section 25.312(7b) [M.S.A. §25.312(7b)]. This is same as Michigan Compiled Laws Annotated, §722.27b. Additional affidavit required.

Effect of adoption: Visitation rights terminate upon adoption unless the adoption is by a stepparent.

Custody statutes: Best interest of child considering: (1) love, affection and other emotional ties existing between the parties and the child; (2) the capacity and disposition of each to give love, affection, guidance and continuation of education and raising the child in its religion; (3) the capacity and disposition of each to provide food, clothing and medical care; (4) length of time the child has lived in a stable, satisfactory environment, and the desirability of maintaining continuity; (5) permanence as a family unit of the existing or proposed custodial home; (6) moral fitness of the parties; (7) mental and physical health of the parties and child; (8) home, school and community record of the child; (9) preference of the child, if of suitable age; (10) willingness and ability of the parties to facilitate and encourage a relationship between the child and the other parent; and (11) any other relevant factor. M.S.A. §25.312(3); M.C.L.A. §722.23. Grandparent or other third party may only get custody if: (1) child's biological parents were never married, and (2) the parent with custody dies or is missing and the other parent has not been granted custody, and (3) the person seeking custody is related within the 5th degree by marriage, blood, or adoption (grandparent or great-grandparent qualifies). M.S.A. §25.312(6c)-(6e); M.C.L.A. §§722.26c-722.26e.

Parental preference: Yes.

MINNESOTA

The law: Minnesota Statutes Annotated. "M.S.A." Ignore volume numbers; look for "section" numbers.

Grandparent visitation: Visitation may be granted: (1) if the grandparents are the parents of a deceased parent of the child; or (2) during or after proceedings for divorce, custody, legal separation, annulment, or paternity. In both situations, it must be determined that visitation is in the child's best interest and will not interfere with the parent-child relationship. M.S.A. §257.022.

Effect of adoption: Visitation rights terminate upon adoption by anyone other than a stepparent or grandparent.

Custody statutes: Factors: (1) wishes of the parties; (2) preference of the child, if of sufficient age; (3) child's primary caretaker; (4) intimacy of the relationship between child and each party; (5) interaction and interrelationship between child and the parties, siblings, and other significant persons; (6) child's adjustment to home, school and community; (7) length of time in a stable, satisfactory environment, and desirability of maintaining continuity; (8) permanence, as a family unit, of the existing or proposed home; (9) mental and physical health of all persons involved; (10) each party's capacity and disposition to give love, affection, and guidance, and to continue educating and raising the child in the child's culture and religion, if any; (11) child's cultural background; (12) effect of any domestic violence on the child; and (13) any other relevant factor. M.S.A. §518.17. See M.S.A. §518.179 for list of criminal acts which prohibit custody.

Parental preference: No.

MISSISSIPPI

The law: Mississippi Code Annotated 1972. "M.C."

Grandparent visitation: When a Mississippi court enters a custody order terminating the rights of a parent, or when a parent dies, the parents of the non-custodial parent or the deceased parent can be awarded visitation. A grandparent who does not qualify as above can petition for visitation if there is a viable relationship between the child and the grandparent, and the grandparent is unreasonably denied access, and the visits are in the child's best interest. A viable relationship is defined as providing financial support, in whole or in part, for six months; or frequent visits, including overnight, for at least one year. Title 93, Section 93-16-1 (M.C. §93-16-1 et. seq.).

Effect of adoption: Visitation rights terminate upon adoption by anyone other than a stepparent or if one of the child's adopted parents was related to the child by blood or marriage before the adoption.

Custody statutes: No statutory factors. Child may choose if at least 12 years of age. Court may require a custody plan from the parties. M.C. §93-13-1 et seq. and 93-23-1 et seq.

Parental preference: Yes.

MISSOURI

The law: Vernon's Annotated Missouri Statutes. "A.M.S." Ignore volume numbers; look for "section" numbers.

Grandparent visitation: Visitation may be granted when the parents of the child have filed for dissolution of their marriage, when one parent of the child is deceased and the surviving parent denies reasonable visitation, or when a grandparent is unreasonably denied visitation with the child for a period of more than ninety days. The court must find that the visitation is in the child's best interest. Chapter 452, Section 452.402 (A.M.S. §452.402).

Effect of adoption: The right of a grandparent to seek or maintain visitation may terminate upon the adoption of the child by someone other than a stepparent, another grandparent, or other blood relative.

Custody statutes: Best interest of child considering: (1) wishes of the parties; (2) wishes of the child; (3) interaction and interrelationship between child and parties, siblings, and other significant persons; (4) child's adjustment to home, school and community; (5) mental and physical health, and any abuse history, of all persons involved; (6) child's needs for continuing relationship with both parties, and the ability and willingness of each to actively perform their duties as mother and father for the needs of the child; (7) any intention of either party to relocate outside the state; (8) which party is more likely to allow frequent and meaningful contact between the child and the other party; and (9) any other relevant factor. A.M.S. §452.375 et seq.

Parental preference: Yes.

MONTANA

The law: Montana Code Annotated. "M.C.A." Ignore volume numbers; look for "title" numbers.

Grandparent visitation: Visitation may be granted in when the court finds that the visitation would be in the child's best interest, including but not limited to a child who is the subject of a disposition made under Title 41. Title 40, Chapter 9, Section 40-9-101 (M.C.A. §40-9-101 et seq.).

Effect of adoption: Visitation rights terminate on adoption by anyone other than a stepparent or a grandparent.

Custody statutes: Factors: (1) parties' wishes; (2) child's wishes; (3) interaction and interrelationship between child and parties, siblings, and other significant persons; (4) child's adjustment to home, school and community; (5) mental and physical condition of all persons involved; (6) any physical abuse, or threat of physical abuse, against a party or the child; (7) any chemical dependency or abuse of either party; (8) the continuity and stability of care; (9) the developmental needs of the child; (10) any adverse effects of the visits on the child; and (11) any other relevant factor. M.C.A. §§40-4-212.

Parental preference: Yes.

NEBRASKA

The law: Revised Statutes of Nebraska 1943. "R.S.N." Ignore volume numbers; look for "chapter" numbers.

Grandparent visitation: Visitation may be granted if at least one of the child's parents is deceased, the marriage of the parents has been dissolved or a petition for dissolution is pending, or if the child's parents have never been married but paternity has been legally established. The court must find that there is a significant beneficial relationship between the grandparents and grandchild and that it would be in the best interest of the child to allow the relationship to continue. The visitation cannot adversely interfere with the parent-child relationship. The grandparent must prove these things by clear and convincing evidence, which is a higher standard or proof than in most civil cases. Chapter 43, Section 43-1801 (R.S.N. 1943 §43-1801 et seq.).

Effect of adoption: Adoption terminates all rights.

Custody statute: Best interest of child considering: (1) relationship of child and each party; (2) reasonable desires of the child; and (3) general health, welfare, and social behavior of child. R.S.N. 1943 §42-364.

Parental preference: Yes.

NEVADA

The law: Nevada Revised Statutes Annotated. "N.R.S.A." Ignore volume numbers; look for "chapter" numbers.

Grandparent visitation: If child's parents are separated or divorced or if one parent is deceased or has relinquished his parental rights or had them terminated, the grandparents and great-grandparents may get visitation if in the best interest of the child. The statute lists specific factors which are to be considered in determining the best interest of the child. Chapter 125A, Section 125A.330 (N.R.S.A. 125A.330).

Effect of adoption: Grandparents can get visitation with a grandchild placed for adoption if the petition for visitation is filed with the court before the date on which the parental rights have been terminated and if the court finds that the visitation would be in the best interest of the child.

Custody statutes: Best interest of the child considering: (1) which party is more likely to allow frequent association and a continuing relationship with the other party; (2) wishes of the child, if of sufficient age and intelligence; (3) "any nomination by a parent of a guardian for the child;" and (4) whether either party has engaged in act of domestic violence against the child, the other party, or other person residing with the child. N.R.S.A. §125.480. See N.R.S.A. §125.510 for required language in decree relating to custody. N.R.S.A. 125.450 et seq.

Parental preference: Yes.

New Hampshire

The law: New Hampshire Statutes Annotated. "N.H.R.S.A." Ignore "title numbers; look for "chapter" numbers.

Grandparent visitation: Visitation may be granted if there is or has been a proceeding under Chapter 458 (for example, for divorce or separation) or if one of the parents is deceased or has had his parental rights terminated, and if the visitation is in the best interest of the child. The best interest is to be determined by using the factors set out in the statute. Grandparents may also be awarded visitation if the child is born out-of-wedlock, provided the child has been legitimated. Chapter 458, Section 458:17-d (N.H.R.S.A. 458:17-d).

Effect of adoption: All rights terminate.

Custody statutes: Factors: (1) preference of child; and (2) any domestic violence. In divorce cases, joint custody is presumed in child's best interest, unless abuse is shown. Decree must state reasons if joint custody is not ordered. N.H.R.S.A. 458:17.

Parental preference: No.

New Jersey

The law: New Jersey Statutes Annotated. "N.J.S.A." Ignore "article" numbers.

Grandparent visitation: Visitation may be granted if is in the best interest of the child, considering: (1) the relationship between the child and the grandparent; (2) the relationship between the parent and the grandparent; (3) the time elapsed since the last contact between the child and the grandparent; (4) the effect visitation will have on the relationship between the child and the custodial parent; (5) if the parents are divorced, the time sharing arrangement between the parents regarding the child; (6) the good faith of the grandparent in filing for visitation; (7) any history of physical, emotional, or sexual abuse or neglect by the grandparent; and (8) any other relevant factor. Title 9, Chapter 2, Section 9:2-7.1 (N.J.S.A.§ 9:2-7.1).

Effect of adoption: All rights terminate unless the adoption is by a stepparent.

Custody statutes: Best interest of the child, considering the following factors: (1) parents' ability to agree, communicate and cooperate in matters relating to the child; (2) parents' willingness to accept custody and facilitate visitation; (3) interaction and interrelationship between the child and parents and siblings; (4) any history of domestic violence; (5) preference of child, if of suitable age; (6) needs of child; (7) stability of home environment offered; (8) quality and continuity of education; (9) fitness of parents; (10) geographical proximity of the parties' homes; (11) extent and quality of time with the child before and after separation; (12) employment responsibilities; and (13) age and number of children. Judge must follow the parties agreement, unless he determines it is not in the child's best interest. Where parties don't agree, judge may require each party to submit a proposed custody plan. N.J.S.A. §§2A:34-23 & 9:2-1 et seq.

Parental preference: Yes.

NEW MEXICO

The law: New Mexico Statutes 1978 Annotated. "N.M.S.A." Ignore volume numbers; look for "chapter" numbers.

Grandparent visitation: Visitation may be granted as part of or subsequent to a judgment of dissolution of the parent's marriage, legal separation, or paternity; if one of the parents is deceased; if the child resided with the grandparent for at least three months and the child was less than six years of age at the beginning of the three month period and was subsequently removed from the grandparent's home; or if the child has resided with the grandparent for a period of at least six months when the child is over the age of six at the beginning of the six month period and the child was subsequently removed from the grandparent's home. Court must consider statutory provisions relating to the best interest of the child. Chapter 40, Section 40-9-1 (N.M.S.A. §40-9-1).

Effect of adoption: Grandparents may obtain visitation after adoption by a stepparent, a relative of the grandchild, a person designated to care for the grandchild in the provisions of a deceased parent's will, or a person who sponsored the grandchild at a baptism or confirmation conducted by a recognized religious organization.

Custody statutes: Best interest of the child, considering: (1) wishes of parties; (2) wishes of child; (3) interaction and interrelationship between the child and parties, siblings and other significant persons; (4) child's adjustment to home, school and community; and (5) mental and physical condition of all persons involved. Other factors are also listed in considering joint custody between parents. N.M.S.A. §40-4-9 et seq.

Parental preference: Yes.

NEW YORK

The law: McKinney's Consolidated Laws of New York Annotated, Domestic Relations Law. "C.L.N.Y., D.R.L." Be sure you use the volumes marked "Domestic Relations."

Grandparent visitation: Visitation may be granted where at least one of the child's parents is deceased or where circumstances show that conditions exist which equity would see fit to intervene. Visitation must also be in the best interest of the child. ***Note:*** There are some court cases that say courts do not generally permit grandparent visitation over the objections of both parents. C.L.N.Y., D.R.L. §72.

Effect of adoption: Visitation can be continued after adoption.

Custody statutes: Best interest of child. No statutory factors. C.L.N.Y., D.R.L. §240.

Parental preference: Yes.

NORTH CAROLINA

The law: General Statutes of North Carolina. "G.S.N.C." Ignore volume numbers; look for "chapter" numbers.

Grandparent visitation: Visitation may be granted as a part of any order determining custody of the child. Chapter 50, Section 50-13.2 (G.S.N.C. §50-13.2).

Effect of adoption: Visitation rights terminate unless the adoption is by a stepparent or a relative of the child where a substantial relationship exists between the grandparent and the child.

Custody statutes: No statutory factors other than best interest of child. G.S.N.C. §50-13 et seq.

Parental preference: Yes.

NORTH DAKOTA

The law: North Dakota Century Code Annotated. "N.D.C.C." Ignore volume numbers; look for "title" numbers.

Grandparent visitation: Grandparents ***must*** be granted visitation upon application (and great-grandparents ***may*** be granted visitation), unless the court determines it would not be in the child's best interest. Visitation is presumed to be in the child's best interest. In deciding best interest, the court must consider the amount of contact between the grandparent, child, and parent. Title 14, Chapter 14-09, Section 14-09-06 (N.D.C.C. §14-09-06).

Effect of adoption: If a grandparent already has visitation rights prior to the adoption, those rights can be terminated upon adoption if found to be in the child's best interest.

Custody statutes: Factors: (1) love, affection and emotional ties between child and each party; (2) each party's capacity and disposition to give love, affection and guidance, and to continue the child's education; (3) each party's disposition to provide food, clothing, medical care and other material needs; (4) length of time the child has been in a stable, satisfactory environment, and the desirability of maintaining continuity; (5) the permanence, as a family unit, of the existing or proposed custodial home; (6) moral fitness of the parties; (7) mental and physical health of the parties; (8) child's home, school and community record; (9) the reasonable preference of the child, if of sufficient intelligence, understanding and experience; (10) any existence of domestic violence; (11) the interaction and interrelationship between the child and parties, siblings and other significant persons; and (12) any other relevant factor. N.D.C.C. §§14-05-22 and 14-09 et seq.

Parental preference: Yes.

OHIO

The law: Page's Ohio Revised Code Annotated. "O.R.C."

Grandparent visitation: Visitation may be granted as a part of or subsequent to the parents' divorce, dissolution of marriage, legal separation, annulment, or child support proceeding if grandparent has an interest in welfare of child and visitation would be in child's best interest. Also if one of the child's parents were never married to each other. If one of the child's parents is deceased, the parent of that parent may seek visitation. Title 31, Section 3109.051 (O.R.C. § 3109.051, 3109.11).

Effect of adoption: Visitation rights terminate upon adoption unless the adoption is by a stepparent.

Custody statutes: Best interest of the child, considering: (1) wishes of parties; (2) child's wishes, if interview by judge; (3) interaction and interrelationship between child and parents, siblings and other significant persons; (4) child's adjustment to home, school and community; (5) mental and physical condition of all persons involved; (6) party more likely to honor and facilitate visitation; (7) compliance with any child support orders; (8) any history of abuse or neglect; (9) any history of visitation denial; and (10) whether a party intends to make his or her residence outside of Ohio. O.R.C. §3109 et seq.

Parental preference: Yes.

OKLAHOMA

The law: Oklahoma Statutes Annotated. "O.S.A."

Grandparent visitation: Visitation may be granted if in the best interest of the child. If child born out of wedlock, father must have been legally determined to be the father for paternal grandparents to obtain visitation. If the child born out of wedlock and parental rights of the father have been terminated, paternal grandparents may get visitation if father has been legally determined to be the father, there was a previous relationship between the child and the grandparents, and visitation would be in the child's best interest. Same true for maternal grandparents if child born out of wedlock and parental rights of mother were terminated. Title 10, Section 5 (10 O.S.A. § 5).

Effect of adoption: If a parent's parental rights have been terminated, the parent of that parent may seek visitation (1) if there is a previous relationship between the grandparent and the grandchild, and (2) if the visits are in the child's best interest.

Custody statutes: Factors: (1) physical, mental and moral welfare of child, and (2) child's preference. It is presumed against child's best interest for party guilty of domestic violence to have custody. 43 O.S.A. §112 et seq.

Parental preference: Yes.

OREGON

The law: Oregon Revised Statutes Annotated. "O.R.S." Ignore volume numbers; look for "chapter" numbers.

Grandparent visitation: Visitation may be granted if (1) the grandparent has established or has attempted to establish ongoing personal contact with the child; and (2) the custodian of the child has denied the grandparent reasonable opportunity to visit the child; and (3) a domestic relations suit is pending. If a final order has been entered in the domestic relations suit, the grandparent must show a change in circumstances since the final order was entered relating to the custodial parent or the child. The visits must also be in the best interest of the child. Chapter 109, Section 109.121 (O.R.S. § 109.121).

Effect of adoption: Visitation rights terminate upon adoption.

Custody statutes: Factors: (1) emotional ties between the child and other family members; (2) each party's interest in and attitude toward the child; (3) desirability of continuing existing relationships; and (4) any abuse of one party by the other. Conduct and lifestyle are only considered if it is causing or may cause emotional or physical damage to the child (this will require strong proof). O.R.S. §§107.105 & 107.137.

Parental preference: Yes.

PENNSYLVANIA

The law: Purdon's Pennsylvania Consolidated Statutes Annotated. "Pa.C.S.A."

Grandparent visitation: Visitation may be granted when at least one of the parents of the child is deceased, when the parents' marriage is dissolved or the parents have been separated for six months or more, or when the child has resided with the grandparents for twelve months or more and is subsequently removed from the home by his parents. The court must find that the visitation is in the best interest of the child and will not interfere with the parent-child relationship and must consider the amount of personal contact between the child and the grandparent prior to the application. If the visitation is based on a deceased parent, only the parents of the deceased parent qualify. If access is sought under the provision where the child has lived with the grandparent for twelve months, the grandparent can seek partial custody. Title 23, Section 5311 (23 Pa.C.S.A. § 5311 et seq.).

Effect of adoption: Visitation rights terminate unless the child is adopted by either a stepparent or grandparents.

Custody statutes: Best interest of child based upon which party is more likely to encourage and allow frequent and continuing contact with the other parent. A grandparent can seek custody if it is in the best interest of the child not to be in the custody of either parent, and is in the best interest of the child for the grandparent to have custody because the grandparent has either assumed the parenting role for at least twelve months or because the child is at substantial risk because of parental abuse, neglect, alcohol or drug abuse, or mental illness. 23 Pa.C.S.A. § 5300 et seq.

Parental preference: Yes.

RHODE ISLAND

The law: 1988 Reenactment of the General Laws of Rhode Island 1956. "G.L.R.I." Ignore "title" and "chapter" numbers; look for "section" numbers.

Grandparent visitation: Visitation may be granted if the court finds that it is in the best interest of the child for the grandparent to be given visitation, that the grandparent is a fit and proper person to have visitation, that the grandparent has repeatedly attempted to visit the grandchild during the six months immediately preceding the filing of the application and was not allowed to visit as a direct result of the actions of either or both of the parents, that there is no other way the grandparent is able to visit the child, and that the grandparent by clear and convincing evidence has successfully rebutted the presumption that the parent's decision to refuse the grandparent visitation was reasonable. Visitation may also be granted if the grandparent's child is deceased or if the child's parents are divorced. G.L.R.I. §15-5-24.1 et seq.

Effect of adoption: Adoption terminates all rights.

Custody statutes: Best interest of child. No statutory factors. G.L.R.I. §15-5-16 et seq.

Parental preference: Yes.

SOUTH CAROLINA

The law: Code of Laws of South Carolina 1976. "C.L.S.C." Ignore volume numbers; look for "title" numbers.

Grandparent visitation: A grandparent may be awarded visitation where one of the parents is deceased, or the parents are divorced or separated. The court must make a written finding that the visits are in the child's best interest and will not cause undue interference The court must consider the nature of the relationship between the child and the grandparents prior to the filing of the request for visitation. Title 20, Section 20-7-420 (C.L.S.C. § 20-7-420).

Effect of adoption: Adoption terminates all rights.

Custody statutes: Determined "...as from the circumstances of the parties and the nature of the case and the best spiritual as well as other interests of the children as may be fit, equitable and just." C.L.S.C. §20-3-160.

Parental preference: No.

SOUTH DAKOTA

The law: South Dakota Codified Laws. "S.D.C.L." Ignore volume numbers; look for "title" numbers.

Grandparent visitation: Visitation may be granted if the child's parents are divorced or legally separated or if an action for divorce or separate maintenance has been commenced by one of the child's parents, or if the grandparent's child has died. The court must find that the visitation is in the child's best interest. Title 25, Chapter 4, Section 25-4-52 (S.D.C.L. §25-4-52 et seq.), 25-4-45.

Effect of adoption: Visitation rights terminate upon adoption unless the adoption is by a stepparent or grandparent.

Custody statutes: Only statutory reference is that custody is to be determined "as may seem necessary and proper." S.D.C.L. §25-4-45.

Parental preference: Yes.

TENNESSEE

The law: Tennessee Code Annotated. "T.C.A." Ignore volume numbers; look for "section" numbers.

Grandparent visitation: [*Special Note:* The Tennessee Supreme Court declared the previous Tennessee grandparent visitation statute unconstitutional. Although the statute has since been changed, it is possible that the new statute has the same constitutional problems as the previous statute. For more information, see "Recent Developments" on page 13.] The statute provides: (1) If one parent is deceased, then the parent of the deceased parent can get visitation; (2) if the parents are divorced or legally separated, any grandparent may request visitation; (3) if the child's parent is missing for at least six months, the parents of the missing parent can seek visitation; (4) if a court in another state has ordered grandparent visitation, those grandparents may seek visitation. The court must find visitation is in the child's best interest, considering the following factors: (1) the length and quality of the prior relationship between the child and the grandparents; (2) the existing emotional ties of the child to the grandparents; (3) the preference of the child; (4) the effect of hostility between the grandparents and parents of the child, manifested before the child, and the willingness of the grandparents, except in cases of abuse, to encourage a close relationship between the child and the parents; and (5) the good faith of the grandparents in filing for visitation. If the child has been removed from the parents' home, the grandparents must also prove that they would adequately protect the child and that they are not implicated in certain specified acts against the child. Title 36, Sections 36-6-302 to 36-6-307 (T.C.A. §§36-6-302 to 36-6-307).

Effect of adoption: Visitation rights terminate upon adoption unless the adoption is by a stepparent or other relative of the child.

Custody statutes: Best interest of child "as the welfare and interest of the child or children may demand." T.C.A. §36-6-101 et seq.

Parental preference: Yes.

TEXAS

The law: Vernon's Texas Codes Annotated. "V.T.C.A."

Grandparent visitation: Visitation may be granted if the grandparent's child has been incarcerated in jail or prison during the three month period preceding the application, has been determined to be legally incompetent, or is dead; if the parents are divorced or have been living apart for the three months period preceding the filing of the application or if a suit for dissolution of the marriage is pending; if the child has been abused or neglected by a parent; the child has been adjudicated to be a child in need of supervision or a delinquent; the grandparent's child has had their parental rights terminated; or if the child has resided with the grandparent for at least six months in the twenty-four month period preceding the filing of the application. The court must find that visits are in the best interest of the child. V.T.C.A., Family Code § 153.433.

Effect of adoption: If the child has been adopted by anyone other than a stepparent, then grandparents cannot petition the court for access to the child.

Custody statutes: Factors: (1) qualifications of the parents; and (2) any evidence of intentional use of abusive force against spouse or any person under age 18 within the past 2 years. V.T.C.A. F.C. §14.01.

Parental preference: Yes.

UTAH

The law: Utah Code Annotated. "U.C." Ignore volume numbers; look for "title" numbers.

Grandparent visitation: Visitation may be granted if the grandparent's child has dies, or has become a non-custodial parent through divorce or legal separation, and it is in the best interest of the child. Title 30, Chapter 5, Section 30-5-1 (U.C. §30-5-1 et seq.). (See also U.C. §30-3-5.)

Effect of adoption: Adoption terminates all rights.

Custody statutes: Best interest of child considering (1) past conduct and demonstrated moral standards of the parties; (2) child's wishes; (3) which party is most likely to act in the child's best interest, including allowing contact with the other party; and (4) any other relevant factor. U.C. §30-3-10.

Parental preference: Yes.

VERMONT

The law: Vermont Statutes Annotated. "V.S.A." Ignore "chapter" numbers; look for "title" numbers.

Grandparent visitation: Visitation may be granted when an action for custody or visitation is or has been considered by the court, or if the grandparent's child is dead, physically or mentally incompetent, or has abandoned the child. The court must find that the visitation is in the child's best interest after considering the statutory factors relating to best interest. Title 15, Section 1011 (15 V.S.A. § 1011 et seq.).

Effect of adoption: Visitation rights terminate unless the child is adopted by a stepparent or a relative of the child.

Custody statutes: Best interest of the child considering: (1) relationship of the child and each party, and each party's ability and disposition to provide love, affection and guidance; (2) ability and disposition to provide food, clothing, medical care, other material needs, and a safe environment; (3) ability and disposition to meet the child's present and future developmental needs; (4) quality of the child's adjustment to present housing, school and community, and potential effect of a change; (5) ability and disposition to foster a continuing relationship with the other party; (6) quality of the child's relationship with the primary caregiver; (7) child's relationship to other significant persons; and (8) ability and disposition of the parties to make joint decisions. 15 V.S.A. §665.

Parental preference: Yes.

VIRGINIA

The law: Code of Virginia 1950 Annotated. "C.V." Ignore "chapter" numbers; look for "title" and "section" numbers.

Grandparent visitation: As a part of a decree dissolving the marriage or a decree that neither party is entitled to a divorce, the court may grant visitation to the grandparent if the grandparent has intervened in the suit for dissolution of the marriage. The court must find that the visitation is in the best interest of the child, after considering the statutory best interest factors. Title 20, Section 20-124.1 (C.V. § 20-124.1).

Effect of adoption: Adoption terminates all rights.

Custody statutes: Best interest of child considering: (1) age, physical and mental condition of the child and parties; (2) relationship between the child and each party; (3) needs of the child; (4) the role each party played, and will play, in the child's upbringing and care; (5) any history of family abuse; and (6) any other relevant factor. C.V. §20-1-7.2. 20-107.2.

Parental preference: Yes.

WASHINGTON

The law: West's Revised Code of Washington Annotated. "R.C.W.A."

Grandparent visitation: [**Special Note:** The Washington Supreme Court has declared the Washington grandparent visitation statute unconstitutional. For more information, see "Recent Developments" on page 13.] When visitation is in the best interest of the child. The grandparent must prove by clear and convincing evidence (this is a higher standard of proof than is require in most civil cases) that a significant relationship exists between the grandparent and the child. Once that is accomplished, then visits will be presumed to be in the child's best interest and the parents will have the burden of overcoming that presumption. Title 26, Chapter 26.09, Section 26.09.240 (R.C.W.A. § 26.09.240).

Effect of adoption: Adoption terminates all rights.

Custody statutes: (1) each party's relative strength, nature and stability of the relationship with the child, including which party has taken greater responsibility for the child; (2) any agreement of the parties; (3) each party's past and potential for future performance of parenting functions; (4) child's emotional needs and development; (5) the child's relationship with siblings and any other significant adults, and involvement in his or her physical surroundings, school, and other activities; (6) the wishes of the parties and the child; and (7) each party's employment schedule. The greatest weight is given to factor (1) above. R.C.W.A. §26.09.187.

Parental preference: Yes.

WEST VIRGINIA

The law: West Virginia Code. "W.V.C." Ignore volume numbers; look for "chapter" numbers.

Grandparent visitation: Grandparents may get visitation when a court orders divorce or separate maintenance and the grandparent's child fails to appear and defend the action or when the whereabouts of that parent are unknown to both the other parent and the grandparent seeking visitation. After a decree of divorce, annulment, paternity, or separate maintenance has been entered, grandparent may petition for visitation when that grandparent's child is the non-custodial parent and that parent has refused, failed, or has been unable to have visitation for a period of six months or more or has been precluded from visitation by a court order or is in the Armed Services and stationed more than one hundred miles from the state border and the grandparent had been refused visitation with the child by the custodial parent for a period of six months or more. A grandparent whose child is deceased may also petition for visitation. Grandparent visitation is also permitted when the child has resided with the grandparent and the parents have resided elsewhere without significant interruption for a period of six consecutive months or more within the previous two year period, the child was removed from the home of the grandparent by the parent, and the removing parent has refused to allow the grandparent visitation. In all cases, the visitation must be found to be in the child's best interest. Chapter 48, Article 2B, Section 48-2B-1 (W.V.C. § 48-2B-1 et seq.).

Effect of adoption: Adoption terminates all rights.

Custody statutes: No statutory factors. Presumption in favor of primary caretaker. W.V.C. §48-2-15.

Parental preference: Yes.

WISCONSIN

The law: West's Wisconsin Statutes Annotated. "W.S.A." Ignore "chapter" numbers; look for "section" numbers.

Grandparent visitation: Visitation may be granted if the grandparent has maintained a relationship with the child similar to the parent-child relationship; the court is to consider the best interest of the child and the wishes of the child. Visitation may also be granted to grandparents if one of the child's parents is deceased and the court finds that the visitation is in the child's best interest. W.S.A. §§880.155 and 767.245.

Effect of adoption: Adoption has no effect on the grandparent's rights if the adoption is by the stepparent.

Custody statutes: Referred to as "legal custody and physical placement." Best interest of the child considering: (1) wishes of parties; (2) wishes of child; (3) interaction and interrelationship between child and the parties, siblings, and any other significant person; (4) child's adjustment to home, school and community; (5) mental and physical health of all parties involved; (6) availability of public or private child care services; (7) whether one party is likely to unreasonably interfere with the child's continuing relationship with the other party; (8) any evidence of child abuse; (9) any evidence of interspousal battery or domestic abuse; (10) whether either party has had a significant problem with alcohol or drug abuse; and (11) any other relevant factor. W.S.A. §767.24.

Parental preference: Yes.

WYOMING

The law: Wyoming Statutes Annotated. "W.S.A." Ignore volume numbers; look for "title" numbers.

Grandparent visitation: Visitation may be granted if it is in the child's best interest and the rights of the child's parents are not substantially impaired. Title 20, Chapter 7, Section 20-7-101 (W.S.A. § 20-7-101).

Effect of adoption: Right terminates upon adoption if neither adopting parent is a natural parent of the child.

Custody statutes: Custody to be determined "...as appears most expedient and beneficial for the well-being of the children. The court shall consider the relative competency of both parents and no award of custody shall be made solely on the basis of gender of the parent." No other statutory factors. W.S.A. §20-2-113.

Parental preference: Yes.

Appendix B
Sample Completed Forms

The forms in this appendix are forms which have been filled in for a fictional case. The purpose is to give you some idea of how the forms look after they have been completed. Not all of the forms in appendix C are included here.

Table of Forms

The following is a list of the forms included in this appendix. These forms have been given letter designations in order to distinguish them from the blank forms in appendix C, which have been given a number instead of a letter. If a form is based on a form from a particular state, the name of the state appears in parentheses after the title of the form. The page number where each form begins is also given.

IN THE CIRCUIT COURT OF THE THIRD JUDICIAL CIRCUIT
IN AND FOR DOUGLAS COUNTY, NEBRASKA

JOHN DOE and JANE DOE

      Petitioners,

VS.   CASE NO._____

ROBERT DOE and WANDA DOE

      Respondents.

COMPLAINT FOR GRANDPARENT VISITATION

      _____JOHN DOE and JANE DOE_____ [hereinafter called the

___Petitioners_____] for ~~his/her~~/their _____Complaint for Grandparent

Visitation_____ against _____ROBERT DOE and WANDA DOE____

_____ [hereinafter called the ___Respondents___], allege(s) and state(s):

1.   Parties.

    The _____Petitioners_____ ~~is~~/are ____paternal grandparents_____,
and reside(s) at ____176 Cornhusker St., Omaha, NE_____.

    The _____Respondents_____ ~~is~~/are _____parents_____,
and reside(s) at ____123 Aksarben Way, Omaha, NE_____.

_____.

    The child(ren) ~~is~~/are ____SARA DOE and SAM DOE_____,

and reside(s) at ____123 Aksarben Way, Omaha, NE_____.

2.   Grounds.

    In support of this request for grandparent visitation, ___Petitioners___ allege(s) and
show(s) the Court as follows: __A petition for dissolution of the Respondents'
marriage is pending, visitation would be in the best interest of the
children and would not interfere with the parent-child relationship.__.

3.   The __Petitioners__ ~~is/~~are not aware of any other court decision, order, or proceeding concerning the custody or visitation of the child(ren) in this state or any other, except:

4.   Relief Requested.

        The _____Petitioners_____ request(s) the following relief from the Court: __Visitation with the children from noon to 6:00 p.m., on the third__ __Sunday of each month, outside of the Respondents' residence.__ .

DATED: __May 19, 1999__

__John Doe__
Signature

__Jane Doe__
Signature

Name: __John Doe__

Address: __176 Cornhusker St.__

    __Omaha, NE 68108__

Telephone: __(402) 555-5555__

Name: __Jane Doe__

Address: __176 Cornhusker St.__

    __Omaha, NE 68108__

Telephone: __(402) 555-5555__

Commonwealth of Massachusetts
The Trial Court
_____Division Probate and Family Court Department Docket No._____

COMPLAINT FOR GRANDPARENT VISITATION

_____JOHN DOE AND JANE DOE_____,
Plaintiffs
v.
_____ROBERT DOE AND WANDA DOE_____,
Defendants

1. Now come the plaintiffs in this action seeking to obtain visitation rights with their grandchildren, namely:

Sam Doe	Date of Birth: 04/01/81
Sara Doe	Date of Birth: 01/12/88

who are unmarried minors and who reside at:_____ 123 Tea Party Way, Boston, MA 02109 _____.

2. Plaintiffs are the _____paternal_____ grandparents who reside at ___1776 Revolution St.,___ Boston, Suffolk County, MA 02109_____.

3. The defendant,_____Wanda Doe_____, who resides at _____123 Tea Party Way, Boston,___ _____Suffolk_____County,_____Massachusetts 02109_____, and the defendant, _____Robert Doe_____, who resides at _____1812 Overture Cir., Boston, Suffolk___ County,_____Massachusetts 02109_____, are the parents of the children.

4. Please check and complete ONLY ONE of the following sections:

☒ a.   On _____October 1, 1992_____, the defendants were divorced by judgment of the Court. The judgment did not provide for visitation rights for the above-named grandparents.

☐ b.   On _____, the defendant father was adjudicated by judgment to be the father of the child(ren). The adjudicated father and mother of the child do not reside together. The judgment/order did not provide for visitation rights for the above-named grandparents.

☐ c.   On _____, the defendants signed an acknowledgment of parentage which was approved by the Court. The parents of the child do not reside together. The order/judgment did not provide for visitation for the above-named grandparents.

☐ d.   The defendants are married but living apart and subject to a temporary order or judgment of separate support. The order/judgment did not provide for visitation for the above-named grandparents.

☐ e.   On _____, _____ died leaving _____ as the surviving parent.

☐ f.   On _____, _____ died and on _____, _____ died. The children currently_____ _____(explain legal status of children).

5. The plaintiffs allege that it is in the best interest of the minor children that they be granted visitation with the said children.

WHEREFORE, plaintiffs request that the Court enter a judgment that provides them with visitation rights.

Date:_____May 23, 1999_____

John Doe
Plaintiff
_____John Doe_____
Print Name

Jane Doe
Plaintiff
_____Jane Doe_____
Print Name
_____1776 Revolution St._____
Street address
_____Boston, MA 02109_____
City or town

Tel. No. _____(617) 555-5555_____

NO. 94-11111

IN THE MATTER OF	*	IN THE DISTRICT COURT
THE MARRIAGE OF	*	
ROBERT DOE		
AND		___999th___ JUDICIAL DISTRICT
WANDA DOE		
AND IN THE INTERESTS OF		
SAM DOE and SARA DOE,		
MINOR CHILDREN		_____BEXAR_____COUNTY, TEXAS

PETITION OF GRANDPARENT(S) FOR INTERVENTION IN SUIT AFFECTING THE PARENT-CHILD RELATIONSHIP

This petition in intervention is brought by _____JOHN DOE and JANE DOE_____.
In support, Intervenors show:

1.   Parties

This suit is brought by _____JOHN DOE_____, whose age is ___65___ years and _____JANE DOE_____, whose age is ___57___ years. Petitioners, who are the ___paternal___ grandparents of the children the subject of this suit, reside at _____ _____1836 Alamo St., San Antonio, TX 78284_____. Petitioners have standing to bring this suit under section 11.03 of the Texas Family Code.

2.   Jurisdiction

No court has continuing jurisdiction of this suit or of the children the subject of this suit.

3.   Children

The following children are the subject of this suit:

NAME: __SAM DOE_____

SEX: ___Male_____

BIRTHPLACE: _San Antonio, TX_____

BIRTH DATE: _April 1, 1985___

PRESENT RESIDENCE: _123 Sam Houston Dr., San Antonio, TX 78284___

NAME: __SARA DOE_____

SEX: ___Female___

BIRTHPLACE: _Houston, TX_____

BIRTH DATE: _January 12, 1992___

PRESENT RESIDENCE: _123 Sam Houston Dr., San Antonio, TX 78284___

4.   Mother

The mother of the children is _____WANDA DOE_____, whose age is over 21 years and whose residence is _123 Sam Houston Dr., San Antonio, TX 78284___.

5.   Father

The father of the children is _____ ROBERT DOE _____, whose age is over 21 years and whose residence is ___ 181 Lone Star, San Antonio, TX 78284 ___.

6.   Court-Ordered Relationships

There are no persons having a court-ordered relationship with the children.

7.   Property

A full description and statement of value of all property owned or possessed by the children is as follows

No property is owned by the children.

8.   Access

It is in the best interest of the children that Petitioners be granted reasonable access to the children by order of this Court.

At the time this relief is requested, Petitioners allege the parents of the children are biologic or adoptive parents.

A suit for the dissolution of the parents' marriage is pending.

The parents of the children have been living apart for the three-month period preceeding the filing of this petition.

Other statutory grounds: _____

Petitioners request the Court to enter its order for access to the children as follows: Grandparents_____
___ ROBERT DOE and JANE DOE ___ are to have possession of the children from
___ 12:00 noon to 5:00 p.m., on the third Sunday of each month. ___.

9.   Prayer

Petitioners prays that citation and notice issue as required by law. Petitioners pray that the Court grant relief in accordance with the foregoing allegations. Petitioners pray for general relief.

Respectfully submitted,

BY:___ *John Doe* ___

Name:___ John Doe ___

BY:___ *Jane Doe* ___

Name:___ Jane Doe ___

Address:___ 1836 Alamo St. ___

___ San Antonio, TX 78284 ___

Telephone:___ (512) 555-5555 ___

CERTIFICATE OF SERVICE

I certify that a true copy of the above was served on ___ Robert Doe, 181 Lone Star, San Antonio, TX 78284; and Wanda Doe, 123 Sam Houston Dr., San Antonio, TX 78283, in accordance with the Texas Rules of Civil Procedure on ___ May 19, 1999 ___.

John Doe

NO. <u>94-11111</u>

IN THE INTEREST OF	*	IN THE DISTRICT COURT
	*	
SAM DOE and	*	<u> 999th </u>DISTRICT COURT
SARA DOE,	*	
	*	
MINOR CHILDREN	*	<u> BEXAR </u>COUNTY, TEXAS

ORIGINAL PETITION FOR GRANDPARENT ACCESS

1. <u>Parties</u>

This suit is brought by <u>   JOHN DOE   </u>, whose age is <u>65</u> years and <u>JANE DOE</u>, whose age is <u>59</u> years. Petitioners, who are the <u>paternal</u> grandparents of the children the subject of this suit, reside at <u>1836 Alamo St., San Antonio, TX 78284</u>. Petitioners have standing to bring this suit under section 11.03 of the Texas Family Code.

2. <u>Jurisdiction</u>

No court has continuing jurisdiction of this suit or of the children the subject of this suit.

3. <u>Children</u>

The following children are the subject of this suit:

NAME:<u>   SAM DOE   </u>

SEX:<u> Male </u>

BIRTHPLACE: <u>San Antonio, TX</u>

BIRTH DATE: <u>April 1, 1981</u>

PRESENT RESIDENCE: <u>123 Sam Houston Dr., San Antonio, TX 78284</u>

NAME: <u>   SARA DOE   </u>

SEX: <u> Female </u>

BIRTHPLACE: <u>San Antonio, TX</u>

BIRTH DATE: <u>January 12, 1988</u>

PRESENCE RESIDENCE: <u>123 Sam Houston Dr., San Antonio, TX 78284</u>

4. <u>Mother</u>

The mother of the children is <u>   WANDA DOE   </u>, whose age is over 21 years and whose residence is: <u>123 Sam Houston Dr., San Antonio, TX 78284</u>.

5. <u>Father</u>

The father of the children is <u>   ROBERT DOE   </u>, whose age is over 21 years and whose residence is:<u>181 Lone Star, San Antonio, TX 78284</u>.

6. <u>Court-Ordered Relationships</u>

There are no persons having a court-ordered relationship with the children.

7. <u>Property</u>

A full description and statement of value of all property owned or possessed by the children is as follows: No property is owned by the children.

8. <u>Access</u>

It is in the best interest of the children that Petitioners be granted reasonable access to the children by order of this Court.

At the time this relief is requested, Petitioners allege the parents of the children are biologic or adoptive parents.

The parents of the children have been living apart for the three-month period preceding the filing of this petition.

Petitioners request the Court to enter its order for access to the children as follows: Grandparents _____ _____ JOHN DOE and JANE DOE _____ are to have possession of the children from 12:00 noon to 8:00 p.m. on the third Sunday of each month, beginning on the third Sunday of June, 1999 _____.

9. <u>Prayer</u>

Petitioners pray that citation and notice issue as required by law. Petitioners pray that the Court grant relief in accordance with the foregoing allegations. Petitioners pray for general relief.

Respectfully submitted,

BY: *John Doe* _____

Name: John Doe _____

BY: *Jane Doe* _____

Name: Jane Doe _____

Address: 1836 Alamo St. _____

San Antonio, TX 78284

Telephone No. (512) 555-5555

IN THE CIRCUIT COURT FOR ANNE ARUNDEL COUNTY, MARYLAND

JOHN DOE and JANE DOE,

　　　　　　　Plaintiffs,

VS.　　　　　　　　　　　　　　　　　　CASE NO. 95-2749

ROBERT DOE and WANDA DOE,

　　　　　　　Defendants.

SUMMONS

TO: Each Sheriff of the State of Maryland

YOU ARE COMMANDED to serve this summons and a copy of the complaint in this action on the Defendant(s):

> Robert Doe and Wanda Doe
> 123 Chesapeake Rd.
> Annapolis, MD 21401

The Defendant(s) is/are required to serve written defenses to the complaint on the Plaintiff(s):

> John Doe and Jane Doe
> 493 Naval Academy Lane
> Annapolis, MD 21401

Within 20 calendar days after this Summons is served on the Defendant(s), exclusive of the day of service, and to file the original of the defenses with the clerk of this court either before service on the Plaintiff(s) or immediately thereafter. If the Defendant fails to do so, a default will be entered against the Defendant for the relief demanded in the complaint.

DATED on _____, _____.

　　　　　　　　　　　　　　Clerk of the Court

By_____

FAYETTE COUNTY CIRCUIT COURT, KENTUCKY

JOHN SMITH and JANE SMITH,

        Petitioners,

VS.   CASE NO. 94-12345

BOB SMITH and SUSAN SMITH,

        Respondents.

MOTION FOR DEFAULT

The undersigned_____Petitioner_____ hereby moves for the entry of a default against the Respondents, Bob and Susan Smith for failure to serve or file a timely response to the ___ Petition for Grandparent Visitation _____ as required by law.

DATED: _June 23, 1999_____

                        *John Smith*_____

                        Signature

                        Name___John Smith_____

                        Address__123 Horse Park Circle_____

                              Lexington, KY 40511_____

                        Telephone No.__(606) 555-5555_____

DEFAULT

A default is entered in this action against the _____ for failure to serve or file a response as required by law.

DATED:_____

                        CLERK OF THE COURT

                        By: _____

IN THE CIRCUIT COURT FOR JEFFERSON COUNTY, ALABAMA

JOHN SMITH and JANE SMITH,
          Plaintiffs,

vs.   Case No. 95-0383

ROBERT SMITH and MARY SMITH,
          Defendants.

WAIVER

STATE OF   **ALABAMA**   )

COUNTY OF   **JEFFERSON**   )

BEFORE ME, the undersigned authority, on this day personally appeared _____**ROBERT SMITH**_____

_____, who, by me duly sworn, made the following statements and swore that they were true:

I, _____**ROBERT SMITH**_____, am the _____**Defendant**_____ in the above-entitled and numbered cause. My mailing address is_____**1421 Jackson Avenue,**_____ **Birmingham, AL 35203** _____.

I have been given a copy of the _____**Complaint for Grandparent Visitation**_____ _____ that has been filed in this cause, and I have read it and understand it. I hereby enter my appearance in this cause for all purposes and waive the issuance and service of process. I agree that the cause may be taken up and considered by the Court without further notice to me. I further waive the making of a record of testimony in this cause.

I further agree that the cause may be heard by the presiding Judge of the Court or by a duly appointed master, hearing officer, or referee of the Court.

Robert Smith
_____

SIGNED under oath before me on_____**September 1, 1999**_____.

C. U. Sine
_____
C. U. Sine
Notary Public
My commission expires: January 1, 2001

NO._____99-11739_____

IN THE INTEREST OF	*	IN THE DISTRICT COURT
SAM DOE and	*	
SARA DOE	*	_____999th_____DISTRICT
CHILDREN	*	_____BEXAR_____ COUNTY, TEXAS

DECREE GRANTING GRANDPARENT ACCESS

On _____August 12, 1999_____, hearing was held in this cause.

<u>Appearances</u>

Petitioners, _____JOHN DOE and JANE DOE_____,
appeared in person.

Respondents, _____ROBERT DOE_____,
appeared in person and through their attorney of record, _____LEE GIL BEIGEL_____.

_____WANDA DOE_____ waived issuance and service of citation by waiver duly filed herein and did not otherwise appear.

<u>Jurisdiction</u>

The Court, having examined the pleadings and heard the evidence and argument of counsel, finds that it has jurisdiction of this cause and of all the parties and that no other court has continuing, exclusive jurisdiction of this cause.

<u>Findings</u>

A jury was waived, and all matters in controversy, including questions of act and of law, were submitted to the Court. All persons entitled to citation were properly cited. The making of a record of testimony was waived by the parties with the consent of the Court.

The Court finds that the children the subject of this suit are:

NAME: _____SAM DOE_____
SEX: _____Male_____
BIRTHPLACE: _____San Antonio, TX_____
BIRTH DATE: _____April 1, 1985_____
PRESENT RESIDENCE: _____123 Sam Houston Dr., San Antonio, TX 78284_____
HOME STATE: _____Texas_____

NAME: _____SARA DOE_____
SEX: _____Female_____
BIRTHPLACE: _____Houston, TX_____
BIRTH DATE: _____Jan. 12, 1992_____
PRESENT RESIDENCE: _____123 Sam Houston Dr., San Antonio, TX 78284_____
HOME STATE: _____Texas_____

<u>Orders</u>

The Court finds that the following orders are in the best interest of the children:

IT IS ORDERED AND DECREED that _____JOHN DOE and JANE DOE_____
are granted access to the children as follows: Grandparents_____JOHN DOE and JANE DOE_____
are to have possession of the children from _____12:00 noon to 8:00 p.m., on the third_____
_____of each month, beginning on the third Sunday of September, 1999_____.

<u>Surrender of Child.</u> _____ROBERT DOE and WANDA DOE_____
are each ORDERED AND DECREED to surrender the child to _____
_____JOHN DOE and JANE DOE_____ at the beginning of each period of
_____JOHN DOE and JANE DOE_____'s possession at the residence of
_____WANDA DOE_____.

<u>Return of Child.</u> _____JOHN DOE and JANE DOE_____
ARE ORDERED AND DECREED to surrender the child to _____WANDA DOE_____
_____ at the end of each period of possession at the
residence of _____WANDA DOE_____.

      <u>Personal Effects</u>. Each party is ORDERED AND DECREED to return with the child the personal effects that the child brought at the beginning of the period of possession.

      <u>Designation of Competent Adult</u>. Each party may designate any competent adult to pick up and return the child, as applicable. IT IS ORDERED AND DECREED that a conservator or a designated competent adult be present when the child is picked up or returned.

Location

      Each party is ORDERED AND DECREED to keep the other party and the Court fully and promptly informed of his or her current street address of residence, home telephone number, name of employer, place of employment, and work telephone number and of the address of the children's school or day-care center. Each party who intends a change of place of residence is ORDERED AND DECREED to give written notice of the intended date of change, new telephone number, and new street address of residence to the Clerk of this Court and every other party who has possession of or access to the children on or before the 60th day before the change of residence or, if the party did not know and could not have known of the change or if the required information is not available within the 60-day period, on or before the fifth day after the day the party knew or should have known of the change or of the related information.

      Notice may be given to the other party by delivering a copy of the notice to the party either in person or by registered or certified mail, return receipt requested, to the party's last known address. Notice may be given to the Court by delivering a copy of the notice either in person to the Clerk of the Court or by registered or certified mail addressed to the Clerk.

WARNINGS TO PARTIES

      FAILURE TO OBEY A COURT ORDER FOR CHILD SUPPORT OR FOR POSSESSION OF OR ACCESS TO A CHILD MAY RESULT IN FURTHER LITIGATION TO ENFORCE THE ORDER, INCLUDING CONTEMPT OF COURT. A FINDING OF CONTEMPT MAY BE PUNISHED BY CONFINEMENT IN JAIL FOR UP TO SIX MONTHS, A FINE OF UP TO $500 FOR EACH VIOLATION, AND A MONEY JUDGMENT FOR PAYMENT OF ATTORNEY'S FEES AND COURT COSTS.

      FAILURE OF A PARTY TO MAKE A CHILD-SUPPORT PAYMENT TO THE PLACE AND IN THE MANNER REQUIRED BY A COURT ORDER MAY RESULT IN THE PARTY'S NOT RECEIVING CREDIT FOR MAKING THE PAYMENT.

      FAILURE OF A PARTY TO PAY CHILD-SUPPORT DOES NOT JUSTIFY DENYING THAT PARTY COURT-ORDERED POSSESSION OF OR ACCESS TO A CHILD. REFUSAL BY A PARTY TO ALLOW POSSESSION OF OR ACCESS TO A CHILD DOES NOT JUSTIFY FAILURE TO PAY COURT-ORDERED CHILD SUPPORT TO THAT PARTY.

      EACH PERSON WHO IS A PARTY TO THIS ORDER OR DECREE IS ORDERED TO NOTIFY THE CLERK OF THIS COURT WITHIN 10 DAYS AFTER THE DATE OF ANY CHANGE IN THE PARTY'S CURRENT RESIDENCE ADDRESS, MAILING ADDRESS, HOME TELEPHONE NUMBER, NAME OF EMPLOYER, ADDRESS OF PLACE OF EMPLOYMENT, OR WORK TELEPHONE NUMBER. ALL NOTICES SHALL BE IN WRITING AND SHALL STATE THE NEW INFORMATION AND THE EFFECTIVE DATE OF THE CHANGE. THE DUTY TO FURNISH THIS INFORMATION TO THE CLERK OF THE COURT CONTINUES AS LONG AS ANY PERSON, BY VIRTUE OF THIS ORDER OR DECREE, IS UNDER AN OBLIGATION TO PAY CHILD SUPPORT OR IS ENTITLED TO POSSESSION OF OR ACCESS TO A CHILD. FAILURE TO OBEY THE ORDER OF THIS COURT TO PROVIDE THE CLERK WITH THE CURRENT MAILING ADDRESS OF A PARTY MAY RESULT IN THE ISSUANCE OF A CAPIAS FOR THE ARREST OF THE PARTY IF THAT PARTY CANNOT BE PERSONALLY SERVED WITH NOTICE OF A HEARING AT AN ADDRESS OF RECORD.

Costs

      Costs of court are to be borne by the party by whom such costs were incurred.

<u>Date of Judgment</u>
      SIGNED on _____, _____ .

                                   _____

                                   JUDGE PRESIDING

APPROVED AS TO FORM ONLY: APPROVED AND CONSENTED TO AS TO
                                      BOTH FORM AND SUBSTANCE:

_____   _____
Attorney for

_____   _____

_____

SUPERIOR COURT OF CALIFORNIA, COUNTY OF ORANGE

JOHN SMITH and JANE SMITH,

     Petitioners,

VS.   CASE NO.95-3481

BOB SMITH and SUSAN SMITH,

     Respondents.

PETITION FOR CHILD CUSTODY

          JOHN SMITH and JANE SMITH   (hereinafter called the __Petitioners__) for his/her/their __Petition for Child Custody__ against __BOB SMITH and SUSAN SMITH__ (hereinafter called the __Respondents__), allege(s) and state(s):

1.   <u>Parties.</u>

    The __Petitioners__ is/are __the maternal grandparents__ , and reside(s) at __6789 Big Sur Drive, Santa Ana, CA 96734__ .

    The __Respondents__ is/are __the parents__ , and reside at __241 Fault Line Blvd., Santa Anna CA__

    The child(ren) is/are __ANN SMITH (DOB 12/12/89 in Dallas, TX), and TOMMY SMITH (DOB 3/5/91 in Lone Pine, CA)__ and reside at __241 Fault Line Blvd., Santa Anna CA__ .

2.   <u>Grounds.</u> In support of this request for physical custody, __Petitioners__ allege(s) and show(s) the Court as follows: __The children's current environment presents a serious threat to the children's physical health and welfare as the Respondents are leaving the children without supervision for extended periods of time, and are not providing the children with adequate medical and dental care.__

3.   The Petitioner(s) is/are not aware of any other court decision, order, or proceeding concerning the custody or visitation of the child(ren) in this state or any other, except:

4.   <u>Relief Requested.</u> The   <u>Petitioners</u>   request(s) the following relief from the Court:

<u>That Petitioners be awarded physical custody of the children</u>

_____

_____.

DATED: <u>September 6, 1999</u>

<u>*John Smith*_____</u>
Signature
Name:<u>   John Smith_____</u>

<u>*Jane Smith*_____</u>
Signature
Name:<u>   Jane Smith_____</u>
Address:<u>   6789 Big Sur Drive_____</u>
<u>   Santa Ana, CA   92711_____</u>
Telephone No.<u>   (714) 555-5555_____</u>

NO._____

IN THE INTEREST OF	*	IN THE DISTRICT COURT
	*	
	*	
SAM DOE and	*	_____999th_____ DISTRICT COURT
SARA DOE,	*	
	*	
	*	
	*	
MINOR CHILDREN	*	_____BEXAR_____ COUNTY, TEXAS

ORIGINAL PETITION IN SUIT
AFFECTING THE PARENT-CHILD RELATIONSHIP

1.   Petitioner.

This suit is brought by _____JOHN DOE and JANE DOE_____,
Petitioner(s), who is/are over 21 years of age and who reside(s) at___1836 Alamo Street,__
__San Antonio, TX 78284_____.

Petitioners are the grandmother and grandfather of the children the subject of this suit.

Petitioners have standing to bring this suit in that Petitioners would show the court that the child's present environment presents a serious and immediate question concerning the child's physical health or welfare.

2.   Jurisdiction.

No court has continuing jurisdiction of this suit or of the children the subject of this suit.

3.   Children.

The following children are the subject of this suit:

NAME: __SAM DOE_____
SEX: __Male_____
BIRTHPLACE: __San Antonio, TX_____
BIRTH DATE: __April 1, 1985_____
PRESENT RESIDENCE: __123 Sam Houston Dr., San Antonio, TX 78284__

NAME: __SARA DOE_____
SEX: __Female_____
BIRTHPLACE: __Houston, TX_____
BIRTH DATE: __January 12, 1988_____
PRESENT RESIDENCE: __123 Sam Houston Dr., San Antonio, TX 78284__

4.   Persons Entitled to Citation.

The mother of the child(ren) is _____WANDA DOE_____, who is over 21 years of age and who resides at _123 Sam Houston Dr., San Antonio, TX 78284_.

Process should be served at that address.

The father of the child(ren) is _____ROBERT DOE_____, who is over 21 years of age and who resides at _181 Lone Star, San Antonio, TX 78284_____.

Process should be served at that address.

There are no court-ordered conservatorships, court-ordered guardianships, or other court-ordered relationship affecting the children the subject of this suit.

5.   Property.

No property is owned or possessed by the children the subject of this suit.

6.   Conservatorship.

The parents of the children are or will be separated. It is in the best interest of the children that the Petitioner be appointed sole managing conservator of the children.

7.   Support.

___ROBERT DOE and WANDA DOE_____, Respondents, are obligated to support the children and should be ordered by the Court to make payments for the support of the children in the manner specified by the Court.

8.   Prayer.

Petitioner prays that citation and notice issue as required by law and that the Court enter its orders in accordance with the foregoing allegations.

Petitioner prays for attorney's fees, expenses, and costs.

Petitioner prays for general relief.

Respectfully submitted,

BY:___*John Doe*_____

Name:____John Doe_____

BY:___*Jane Doe*_____

Name:____Jane Doe_____

Address:___1836 Alamo St._____

___San Antonio, TX 78284_____

Telephone:___(512) 555-5555_____

IN THE CIRCUIT COURT OF THE THIRD JUDICIAL DISTRICT

COOK COUNTY, ILLINOIS

PAULA SMITH and PETER SMITH

Petitioners,

VS.   CASE NO. 95-32946

ROBERT JONES and REBA JONES,

Respondents.

SUBPOENA

DUCES TECUM

TO: ED U. KATER
Northside Elementary School
1427 Northside Blvd.
Chicago, IL 60607

YOU ARE HEREBY COMMANDED to appear before the Honorable _____

___Barry D. Hatchett_____, Judge of the Court, at __Courtroom C,_____

__Cook County Courthouse, 251 Michigan Ave., Chicago, IL_____,
on _____October 22_____, _1999__, at _9:00____ o'clock _A_.M., to testify in this action.
You are also commended to bring with you the following:

Any and all report cards, grade books, or other school records
relating to Robert Jones, Jr.

If you fail to appear, you may be in contempt of court.

You are subpoenaed to appear by the attorneys or parties designated below, and unless excused from this subpoena by these attorneys or parties, or the court, you shall respond to this subpoena as directed.

DATED:_____

Attorney or Party Requesting Subpoena   CLERK OF THE COURT

Name: _Paula Smith_____

Address: __6932 Lakeshore Cir._____

_____Chicago, IL 60607_____   By: _____
Telephone No: __(312) 555-5515_____   Deputy Clerk

STATE OF MINNESOTA DISTRICT COURT

COUNTY OF HENNEPIN, FIRST JUDICIAL DISTRICT

GEORGE BROWN,

        Petitioner,

vs.   CASE NO. 95-2393

GEORGE BROWN, JR., and SUSAN BROWN,

        Respondents.

NOTICE OF HEARING

TO: GEORGE BROWN, JR. and SUSAN BROWN
           6693 Martin Rd.
           Minneapolis, MN 55401

PLEASE TAKE NOTICE that the above-entitled matter will be called on for hearing on the Petition for Grandparent Visitation on Tuesday, the 16th day of March, 1999, at 1:30 o'clock P.M., before the Honorable I. M. deJudge, Judge, in his chambers at the Hennepin County Courthouse, 417 Oak Street, 4th Floor, Minneapolis, MN.

George Brown

Signature

Name: George Brown

Address: 4435 S. Mountain View Ave.

Minneapolis, MN 55401

Telephone No. (612) 555-5155

CIRCUIT COURT OF RALEIGH COUNTY, WEST VIRGINIA

JOHN DAVIS and BARBARA DAVIS,
                    Plaintiffs,

vs.   CASE NO. 95-8392

SAM DAVIS and GAIL DAVIS,
                    Defendants.

CUSTODY DECREE

This action for child custody was heard before the Court on _____May 10, 1999_____.
All interested parties appearing were given the opportunity to be heard and to present evidence.
On the evidence presented, the Court makes the following findings and orders:

Jurisdiction

The Court, having examined the pleadings and heard the evidence and argument of the
parties, finds that it has jurisdiction of this cause and of all the parties and that no other court has
continuing, exclusive jurisdiction of this cause. All persons entitled to notice of this action and
final hearing were properly given notice.

Custody

IT IS ORDERED that __the Plaintiffs, JOHN DAVIS and BARBARA DAVIS__

_____ shall have physical custody of the following child(ren):

Sam Davis, Jr., DOB: 2/14/97

The court finds that Defendant's home environment is not in the
best interest of the minor child at the present time, due to
the alcohol addiction of Defendant Sam Davis, and recent inci-
dents of domestic violence which led to proceedings being initiated pursuant to W.V.C. §48-2A-1. The court further finds
that a transfer of custody to the Plaintiffs is in the best
interest of the child, and Plaintiffs are the child's paternal
grandparents, have developed a significant relationship with the
child, and can offer a suitable home environment as indicated
by the home study conducted in this matter.

Visitation

IT IS ORDERED that ___the Defendants, SAM DAVIS and GAIL DAVIS___

_____ shall have visitation with the child(ren) as follows:

alternative Saturdays, from 9:00 a.m. to 6:00 p.m., provided
that another adult be present during all visitation periods.

Child Support

IT IS ORDERED that ___the Defendants, SAM DAVIS and GAIL DAVIS___
shall pay child support in the amount of $___55.00___ per ___week___, to
___the Plaintiffs, JOHN DAVIS and BARBARA DAVIS___.

Costs

Costs of court are to be borne by ___the Plaintiffs___.

Other Provisions

This matter may be reviewed after a period of ninety days, upon
motion of the Defendants, or upon Defendant Sam Davis having
successfully completed a licensed alcohol treatment program,
whichever occurs first.

ORDERED on _____, _____ .

_____
Judge

APPENDIX C
FORMS

The following forms are included in this appendix. These forms are of a general nature, except where a specific state is noted. Therefore, you may need to modify these forms for use in your state. These forms are not in any particular order, and you will not need to use all of the forms in this appendix.

TABLE OF FORMS

_____ [hereinafter called the

_____] for his/her/their_____

_____against _____

_____[hereinafter called the _____], alleges and states:

1.   <u>Parties</u>.

    The _____ is/are _____,
and reside(s) at _____.

    The _____ is/are _____,
and reside(s) at _____.

    The child(ren) is/are _____,
and reside(s) at _____.

2.   <u>Grounds.</u>

    In support of this request for grandparent visitation, _____ allege(s) and
show(s) the Court as follows:_____

_____

_____

_____

_____.

3.   The _____ is/are not aware of any other court decision, order, or proceeding concerning the custody or visitation of the child(ren) in this state or any other, except:

4.   Relief Requested.

The _____ request(s) the following relief from the Court:

_____

_____

_____

_____.

DATED:_____

_____   _____
Signature   Signature

Name:_____   Name:_____

Address:_____   Address:_____

_____   _____

Telephone:_____   Telephone:_____

IN THE CIRCUIT COURT OF THE _____ JUDICIAL CIRCUIT,
IN AND FOR _____ COUNTY, FLORIDA

Case No.: _____
Division: _____

_____ ,

_____ ,
          Grandparent(s),

and

_____ ,

_____ ,
          Respondent(s).

PETITION FOR GRANDPARENT VISITATION

I/We, {full legal name(s)}_____ ,
being sworn, certify that the following information is true:

1. This is a request for grandparent(s) visitation, under chapter 752, Florida Statutes.

2. The minor grandchild(ren) has (have) been living in the State of Florida within the jurisdiction of this Court.

3. I/We desire visitation with the following minor grandchild(ren).

Name	Birth date	Age	Sex

4. The [√ one only] ( ) mother ( ) father of my (our) grandchild(ren) is my (our) [√ one only] ( ) son ( ) daughter. A copy of the my (our) child's (respondent's) birth certificate is attached.

5. [√ all that apply]:
____ a. The ( ) mother ( ) father of the grandchild(ren) has (have) died.
____ b. The mother and father of the grandchild(ren) are divorced.
____ c. The ( ) mother ( ) father of the grandchild(ren) has (have) deserted the grandchild(ren).
____ d. The parents were not married when the grandchild(ren) was (were) born and did not marry after the grandchild(ren)'s birth, and paternity has been established.

6. I/We are requesting the following visitation: {explain} _____
_____
_____
_____

7.   It is in the best interests of the grandchild(ren) that the grandparent(s) be allowed reasonable rights of visitation with the grandchild(ren). This is in the grandchild(ren)'s best interests because: {explain}

_____
_____
_____
_____
_____
_____
_____

I understand that I am swearing or affirming under oath to the truthfulness of the claims made in this petition and that the punishment for knowingly making a false statement includes fines and/or imprisonment.

Dated: _____

_____
Signature of Grandparent
Printed Name: _____
Address: _____
City, State, Zip: _____
Telephone Number: _____
Fax Number: _____

STATE OF FLORIDA
COUNTY OF _____

Sworn to or affirmed and signed before me on _____ by _____.

_____
NOTARY PUBLIC—STATE OF FLORIDA

_____
[Print, type, or stamp commissioned name of notary.]

____   Personally known
____   Produced identification
        Type of identification produced _____

IF A NONLAWYER HELPED YOU FILL OUT THIS FORM, HE/SHE MUST FILL IN THE BLANKS BELOW: [✍ fill in **all** blanks]

I, {full legal name and trade name of nonlawyer}_____,
a nonlawyer, located at {street}_____, {city} _____,
{state} _____, {phone} _____, helped {name} _____,
who is the (one of the) petitioner(s), fill out this form.

Florida Family Law Form 12.905, Petition for Grandparent Visitation (2/98)

I understand that I am swearing or affirming under oath to the truthfulness of the claims made in this petition and that the punishment for knowingly making a false statement includes fines and/or imprisonment.

Dated: _____

_____
Signature of Grandparent

Printed Name: _____

Address: _____

City, State, Zip: _____

Telephone Number: _____

Fax Number: _____

STATE OF FLORIDA
COUNTY OF _____

Sworn to or affirmed and signed before me on _____ by _____.

_____
NOTARY PUBLIC—STATE OF FLORIDA

_____
[Print, type, or stamp commissioned name of notary.]

____ Personally known
____ Produced identification
Type of identification produced _____

IF A NONLAWYER HELPED YOU FILL OUT THIS FORM, HE/SHE MUST FILL IN THE BLANKS BELOW: [✍ fill in **all** blanks]

I, {full legal name and trade name of nonlawyer}_____,
a nonlawyer, located at {street}_____, {city} _____,
{state} _____, {phone} _____, helped {name} _____,
who is the (one of the) petitioner(s), fill out this form.

Commonwealth of Massachusetts
The Trial Court
_____Division Probate and Family Court Department Docket No._____

COMPLAINT FOR GRANDPARENT VISITATION

_____,
Plaintiffs
v.
_____,
Defendants

1. Now come the plaintiffs in this action seeking to obtain visitation rights with their grandchildren, namely:

who are unmarried minors and who reside at: _____.

2. Plaintiffs are the _____ grandparents who reside at _____
_____.

3. The defendant, _____, who resides at _____
_____ County, _____, and the defendant,
_____, who resides at _____
County, _____, are the parents of the children.

4. Please check and complete ONLY ONE of the following sections:

☐ a.   On _____, the defendants were divorced by judgment of the Court. The judgment
did not provide for visitation rights for the above-named grandparents.

☐ b.   On _____, the defendant father was adjudicated by judgment to be the father of
the child(ren). The adjudicated father and mother of the child do not reside together. The judgment/order
did not provide for visitation rights for the above-named grandparents.

☐ c.   On _____, the defendants signed an acknowledgment of parentage which was
approved by the Court. The parents of the child do not reside together. The order/judgment did not provide
for visitation for the above-named grandparents.

☐ d.   The defendants are married but living apart and subject to a temporary order or judgment of separate
support. The order/judgment did not provide for visitation for the above-named grandparents.

☐ e.   On _____, _____ died leaving
_____ as the surviving parent.

☐ f.   On _____, _____ died and on
_____, _____ died. The children
currently_____
_____(explain legal status of children).

5. The plaintiffs allege that it is in the best interest of the minor children that they be granted visitation with the
said children.

WHEREFORE, plaintiffs request that the Court enter a judgment that provides them with visitation rights.

Date:_____

_____   _____
Plaintiff   Plaintiff

_____   _____
Print Name   Print Name

                                             _____
                                             Street address

                                             _____
                                             City or town

                                             Tel. No. _____

NO. _____

IN THE INTEREST OF	*	IN THE DISTRICT COURT
	*	
	*	_____DISTRICT COURT
	*	
	*	
	*	
MINOR CHILDREN	*	_____ COUNTY, TEXAS

ORIGINAL PETITION FOR GRANDPARENT ACCESS

1. <u>Parties</u>

This suit is brought by _____, whose age is _____ years and _____, whose age is _____ years. Petitioners, who are the _____ grandparents of the children the subject of this suit, reside at _____ _____. Petitioners have standing to bring this suit under section 11.03 of the Texas Family Code.

2. <u>Jurisdiction</u>

No court has continuing jurisdiction of this suit or of the children the subject of this suit.

3. <u>Children</u>

The following children are the subject of this suit:

NAME: _____

SEX: _____

BIRTHPLACE: _____

BIRTH DATE: _____

PRESENT RESIDENCE: _____

NAME: _____

SEX: _____

BIRTHPLACE: _____

BIRTH DATE: _____

PRESENT RESIDENCE: _____

4. <u>Mother</u>

The mother of the children is _____, whose age is over 21 years and whose residence is: _____.

5. <u>Father</u>

The father of the children is _____, whose age is over 21 years and whose residence is: _____.

6. <u>Court-Ordered Relationships</u>

There are no persons having a court-ordered relationship with the children.

7.   Property

A full description and statement of value of all property owned or possessed by the children is as follows: No property is owned by the children.

8.   Access

It is in the best interest of the children that Petitioners be granted reasonable access to the children by order of this Court.

At the time this relief is requested, Petitioners allege the parents of the children are biologic or adoptive parents.

A suit for the dissolution of the parents' marriage is pending.

The parents of the children have been living apart for the three-month period preceding the filing of this petition.

Other statutory grounds: _____
_____.

Petitioners request the Court to enter its order for access to the children as follows: Grandparents _____
_____ are to have possession of the children from _____
_____.

9.   Prayer

Petitioners prays that citation and notice issue as required by law. Petitioners pray that the Court grant relief in accordance with the foregoing allegations. Petitioners pray for general relief.

Respectfully submitted,

BY:_____

Name: _____

BY:_____

Name: _____

Address: _____

_____

Telephone: _____

NO. _____

IN THE MATTER OF	*	IN THE DISTRICT COURT
THE MARRIAGE OF		
	*	
AND	*	_____DISTRICT COURT
AND IN THE INTERESTS OF		
	*	
MINOR CHILDREN	*	_____ COUNTY, TEXAS

PETITION OF GRANDPARENT(S) FOR INTERVENTION IN SUIT AFFECTING THE PARENT-CHILD RELATIONSHIP

This petition in intervention is brought by _____.
In support, Intervenors show:

1.   Parties

        This suit is brought by _____, whose age is _____ years
and _____, whose age is _____ years. Petitioners, who are
the _____ grandparents of the children the subject of this suit, reside at _____
_____. Petitioners have standing to
bring this suit under section 11.03 of the Texas Family Code.

2.   Jurisdiction

        No court has continuing jurisdiction of this suit or of the children the subject of this suit.

3.   Children

        The following children are the subject of this suit:

        NAME: _____

        SEX: _____

        BIRTHPLACE: _____

        BIRTH DATE: _____

        PRESENT RESIDENCE: _____

        NAME: _____

        SEX: _____

        BIRTHPLACE: _____

        BIRTH DATE: _____

        PRESENT RESIDENCE: _____

4.   Mother

        The mother of the children is _____, whose age is over
21 years and whose residence is: _____.

151

5. <u>Father</u>

The father of the children is _____, whose age is over 21 years and whose residence is: _____.

6. <u>Court-Ordered Relationships</u>

There are no persons having a court-ordered relationship with the children.

7. <u>Property</u>

A full description and statement of value of all property owned or possessed by the children is as follows:
No property is owned by the children.

8. <u>Access</u>

It is in the best interest of the children that Petitioners be granted reasonable access to the children by order of this Court.

At the time this relief is requested, Petitioners allege the parents of the children are biologic or adoptive parents.

A suit for the dissolution of the parents' marriage is pending.

The parents of the children have been living apart for the three-month period preceding the filing of this petition.

Other statutory grounds: _____ _____.

Petitioners request the Court to enter its order for access to the children as follows: Grandparents _____ _____ are to have possession of the children from _____.

9. <u>Prayer</u>

Petitioners prays that citation and notice issue as required by law. Petitioners pray that the Court grant relief in accordance with the foregoing allegations. Petitioners pray for general relief.

Respectfully submitted,

BY:_____

Name: _____

BY:_____

Name: _____

Address: _____

_____

Telephone: _____

CERTIFICATE OF SERVICE

I certify that a true copy of the above was served on _____ _____,

in accordance with the Texas Rules of Civil Procedure on _____.

_____

UNIFORM CHILD CUSTODY JURISDICTION ACT AFFIDAVIT

1. The name and present address of each child (under 18) in this case is:

2. The places where the child(ren) has/have lived within the last 5 years are:

3. The name(s) and present address(es) of custodians with whom the child(ren) has/have lived within the past 5 years are:

4. I do not know of, and have not participated (as a party, witness, or in any other capacity) in, any other court decision, order, or proceeding (including divorce, separate maintenance, child neglect, dependency, or guardianship) concerning the custody or visitation of the child(ren) in this state or any other state, except:
   [specify case name and number and court's name and address].

5. I do not have information of any pending proceeding (including divorce, separate maintenance, child neglect, dependency, or guardianship) concerning the custody or visitation of the child(ren), in this state or any other state except: [specify case name and number and court's name and address].

       That proceeding _____is continuing _____has been stayed by the court.

       _____Temporary action by this court is necessary to protect the child(ren) because the child(ren) has/have been subjected to or threatened with mistreatment or abuse or is/are otherwise neglected or dependent.
Attach explanation.

6. I do not know of any person who is not already a party to this proceeding who has physical custody of, or who claims to have custody or visitation rights with, the child(ren), except: [state name(s) and address(es)].

7. The child(ren)'s "home state" is _____ ["Home State" means the state in which the child(ren) immediately preceding the time involved lived with his or her parents, a parent, or a person acting as a parent, for at least 6 consecutive months, and, in the case of a child less than 6 months old, the state in which the child lived from birth with any of the persons mentioned. Periods of temporary absence of the named persons are counted as a part of the 6 month or other period.]

I acknowledge a continuing duty to advise this court of any custody or visitation proceeding (including dissolution of marriage, separate maintenance, child neglect, or dependency) concerning the child(ren) in this state or any other state about which information is obtained during this proceeding.

DATED:_____

                        _____

                        Signature of Affiant

                        Name_____

                        Address_____

                        _____

                        Telephone No._____

     Acknowledged before me on _____, by _____
_____, who is personally known to me or produced _____ as identification, and who did take an oath.

                        _____
                        NOTARY PUBLIC
                        My Commission Expires:

CERTIFICATE OF SERVICE

I HEREBY CERTIFY that a true copy of _____

_____

was: _____mailed _____hand delivered to the parties listed below, this _____ day of

_____, _____.

Name_____   Name_____

Address_____   Address_____

_____   _____

Telephone No._____   Telephone No._____

_____

Signature of Party serving document

Name_____

Address_____

_____

Telephone No._____

MOTION FOR DEFAULT

The undersigned _____ hereby moves for the entry of a
default against _____ for failure to serve or file a
timely response to the _____ as
required by law.

DATED: _____

_____
Signature

Name_____

Address_____

_____

Telephone No._____

DEFAULT

A default is entered in this action against _____
for failure to serve or file a response as required by law.

DATED:_____

CLERK OF THE COURT

By: _____

SUBPOENA

TO:

    YOU ARE HEREBY COMMANDED to appear before the Honorable _____ _____, Judge of the Court, at _____ _____, on _____, _____, at _____ o'clock ___.M., to testify in this action. You are also commended to bring with you the following:

    If you fail to appear, you may be in contempt of court.

    You are subpoenaed to appear by the attorneys or parties designated below, and unless excused from this subpoena by these attorneys or parties, or the court, you shall respond to this subpoena as directed.

DATED:_____

                                CLERK OF THE COURT

Attorney or Party Requesting Subpoena
Name: _____
Address: _____   By: _____
          _____
Telephone No: _____

NOTICE OF HEARING

TO:

PLEASE TAKE NOTICE that the above-entitled matter will be called on for hearing on
_____on
_____, the _____ day of _____, _____, at _____ o'clock
_____.M., before the Honorable _____, Judge, at
_____
_____.

_____
Signature

Name:_____

Address:_____

_____

Telephone No._____

_____

VS.   CASE NO. _____

_____

REQUEST FOR MEDIATION

This Request for Mediation is brought by _____, _____.
In support, _____ shows:

There is a reasonable expectation that the dispute in this case may be resolved by the use of mediation.

_____ requests the Court to refer this dispute for resolution by mediation.

_____ prays that the Court grant this Request for Mediation.

_____
SIGNATURE

_____
NAME

_____
ADDRESS

_____
TELEPHONE NUMBER

ORDER ON REQUEST FOR MEDIATION

On _____, the Court considered the Request for Mediation of _____, _____, and finds that the Request should be granted.

IT IS THEREFORE ORDERED that the Request for Mediation of _____, _____, is GRANTED.

IT IS ORDERED that the pending dispute be referred to mediation.

SIGNED on _____, _____.

_____
Judge

WAIVER

STATE OF   )

COUNTY OF   )

     BEFORE ME, the undersigned authority, on this day personally appeared _____

_____, who, by me duly sworn, made the following statements

and swore that they were true:

     I, _____, am the _____ in the

above-entitled and numbered cause. My mailing address is_____

_____.

I have been given a copy of the _____

_____ that has been filed in this cause, and

I have read it and understand it. I hereby enter my appearance in this cause for all purposes and waive the issuance

and service of process. I agree that the cause may be taken up and considered by the Court without further notice

to me. I further waive the making of a record of testimony in this cause.

     I further agree that the cause may be heard by the presiding Judge of the Court or by a duly appointed

master, hearing officer, or referee of the Court.

                                  _____

     SIGNED under oath before me on_____.

                                  _____

                                  Notary Public
                                  My commission expires:

This action for child custody was heard before the Court on _____.
All interested parties appearing were given the opportunity to be heard and to present evidence.
On the evidence presented, the Court makes the following findings and orders

Jurisdiction: The Court, having examined the pleadings and heard the evidence and argument of the parties, finds that it has jurisdiction of this cause and of all the parties and that no other court has continuing, exclusive jurisdiction of this cause. All persons entitled to notice of this action and final hearing were properly given notice.

Visitation:

IT IS ORDERED that_____
shall have visitation with the children, _____
as follows:

Costs: Costs of court are to be borne by _____.

ORDERED on _____, _____.

_____
Judge

NO._____

IN THE INTEREST OF	*	IN THE DISTRICT COURT
	*	
	*	_____DISTRICT
	*	
	*	
	*	
CHILDREN	*	_____ COUNTY, TEXAS

<u>DECREE GRANTING GRANDPARENT ACCESS</u>

On _____, hearing was held in this cause.

<u>Appearances</u>

Petitioners, _____,
appeared in person.

Respondents, _____,
appeared in person and through their attorney of record, _____.
_____ waived issuance and service of citation by
waiver duly filed herein and did not otherwise appear.

<u>Jurisdiction</u>

The Court, having examined the pleadings and heard the evidence and argument of counsel, finds that it has jurisdiction of this cause and of all the parties and that no other court has continuing, exclusive jurisdiction of this cause.

<u>Findings</u>

A jury was waived, and all matters in controversy, including questions of fact and of law, were submitted to the Court. All persons entitled to citation were properly cited. The making of a record of testimony was waived by the parties with the consent of the Court.

The Court finds that the children the subject of this suit are:

NAME: _____
SEX: _____
BIRTHPLACE: _____
BIRTH DATE: _____
PRESENT RESIDENCE: _____
HOME STATE: _____

NAME: _____
SEX: _____
BIRTHPLACE: _____
BIRTH DATE: _____
PRESENT RESIDENCE: _____
HOME STATE: _____

<u>Orders</u>

The Court finds that the following orders are in the best interest of the children:

IT IS ORDERED AND DECREED that _____
are granted access to the children as follows: Grandparents_____
are to have possession of the children from _____
_____.

    <u>Surrender of Child.</u> _____
are each ORDERED AND DECREED to surrender the child to _____
_____ at the beginning of each period of
_____'s possession at the residence of _____
_____.

    <u>Return of Child.</u> _____
ARE ORDERED AND DECREED to surrender the child to _____
_____ at the end of each period of possession at the
residence of _____.

Personal Effects. Each party is ORDERED AND DECREED to return with the child the personal effects that the child brought at the beginning of the period of possession.

Designation of Competent Adult. Each party may designate any competent adult to pick up and return the child, as applicable. IT IS ORDERED AND DECREED that a conservator or a designated competent adult be present when the child is picked up or returned.

Location

Each party is ORDERED AND DECREED to keep the other party and the Court fully and promptly informed of his or her current street address of residence, home telephone number, name of employer, place of employment, and work telephone number and of the address of the children's school or day-care center. Each party who intends a change of place of residence is ORDERED AND DECREED to give written notice of the intended date of change, new telephone number, and new street address of residence to the Clerk of this Court and every other party who has possession of or access to the children on or before the 60th day before the change of residence or, if the party did not know and could not have known of the change or if the required information is not available within the 60-day period, on or before the fifth day after the day the party knew or should have known of the change or of the related information.

Notice may be given to the other party by delivering a copy of the notice to the party either in person or by registered or certified mail, return receipt requested, to the party's last known address. Notice may be given to the Court by delivering a copy of the notice either in person to the Clerk of the Court or by registered or certified mail addressed to the Clerk.

WARNINGS TO PARTIES

FAILURE TO OBEY A COURT ORDER FOR CHILD SUPPORT OR FOR POSSESSION OF OR ACCESS TO A CHILD MAY RESULT IN FURTHER LITIGATION TO ENFORCE THE ORDER, INCLUDING CONTEMPT OF COURT. A FINDING OF CONTEMPT MAY BE PUNISHED BY CONFINEMENT IN JAIL FOR UP TO SIX MONTHS, A FINE OF UP TO $500 FOR EACH VIOLATION, AND A MONEY JUDGMENT FOR PAYMENT OF ATTORNEY'S FEES AND COURT COSTS.

FAILURE OF A PARTY TO MAKE A CHILD-SUPPORT PAYMENT TO THE PLACE AND IN THE MANNER REQUIRED BY A COURT ORDER MAY RESULT IN THE PARTY'S NOT RECEIVING CREDIT FOR MAKING THE PAYMENT.

FAILURE OF A PARTY TO PAY CHILD-SUPPORT DOES NOT JUSTIFY DENYING THAT PARTY COURT-ORDERED POSSESSION OF OR ACCESS TO A CHILD. REFUSAL BY A PARTY TO ALLOW POSSESSION OF OR ACCESS TO A CHILD DOES NOT JUSTIFY FAILURE TO PAY COURT-ORDERED CHILD SUPPORT TO THAT PARTY.

EACH PERSON WHO IS A PARTY TO THIS ORDER OR DECREE IS ORDERED TO NOTIFY THE CLERK OF THIS COURT WITHIN 10 DAYS AFTER THE DATE OF ANY CHANGE IN THE PARTY'S CURRENT RESIDENCE ADDRESS, MAILING ADDRESS, HOME TELEPHONE NUMBER, NAME OF EMPLOYER, ADDRESS OF PLACE OF EMPLOYMENT, OR WORK TELEPHONE NUMBER. ALL NOTICES SHALL BE IN WRITING AND SHALL STATE THE NEW INFORMATION AND THE EFFECTIVE DATE OF THE CHANGE. THE DUTY TO FURNISH THIS INFORMATION TO THE CLERK OF THE COURT CONTINUES AS LONG AS ANY PERSON, BY VIRTUE OF THIS ORDER OR DECREE, IS UNDER AN OBLIGATION TO PAY CHILD SUPPORT OR IS ENTITLED TO POSSESSION OF OR ACCESS TO A CHILD. FAILURE TO OBEY THE ORDER OF THIS COURT TO PROVIDE THE CLERK WITH THE CURRENT MAILING ADDRESS OF A PARTY MAY RESULT IN THE ISSUANCE OF A CAPIAS FOR THE ARREST OF THE PARTY IF THAT PARTY CANNOT BE PERSONALLY SERVED WITH NOTICE OF A HEARING AT AN ADDRESS OF RECORD.

Costs

Costs of court are to be borne by the party by whom such costs were incurred.

Date of Judgment

SIGNED on _____, _____.

_____
JUDGE PRESIDING

APPROVED AS TO FORM ONLY: APPROVED AND CONSENTED TO AS TO
                                             BOTH FORM AND SUBSTANCE:

_____   _____
Attorney for

                                             _____
_____

_____

_____ (hereinafter called the
_____) for his/her/their _____
against _____ (hereinafter called the
_____), allege(s) and state(s):

1.   Parties.

The _____ is/are _____, and
reside(s) at _____.

The _____ is/are _____, and
reside at_____
_____.

The child(ren) is/are_____
_____ and
reside at_____.

2.   Grounds. In support of this request for physical custody, _____
allege(s) and show(s) the Court as follows: _____
_____
_____
_____
_____.

3.	The Petitioner(s) is/are not aware of any other court decision, order, or proceeding concerning the custody or visitation of the child(ren) in this state or any other, except:

4.	<u>Relief Requested.</u> The _____ request(s) the following relief from the Court:

_____

_____

_____.

DATED: _____

_____
Signature
Name:_____

_____
Signature
Name:_____
Address:_____

_____
Telephone No._____

NO._____

IN THE INTEREST OF

          *   IN THE DISTRICT COURT

          *

          *

          *   _____ DISTRICT COURT

          *

          *

          *

MINOR CHILDREN

          *   _____ COUNTY, TEXAS

ORIGINAL PETITION IN SUIT
AFFECTING THE PARENT-CHILD RELATIONSHIP

1.   <u>Petitioner</u>.

This suit is brought by _____,
Petitioner(s), who is/are over 21 years of age and who reside(s) at_____
_____.

Petitioners are the grandmother and grandfather of the children the subject of this suit.

Petitioners have standing to bring this suit in that Petitioners would show the court that the child's present environment presents a serious and immediate question concerning the child's physical health or welfare.

2.   <u>Jurisdiction</u>.

No court has continuing jurisdiction of this suit or of the children the subject of this suit.

3.   <u>Children</u>.

The following children are the subject of this suit:

NAME: _____

SEX: _____

BIRTHPLACE: _____

BIRTH DATE: _____

PRESENT RESIDENCE: _____

NAME: _____

SEX: _____

BIRTHPLACE: _____

BIRTH DATE: _____

PRESENT RESIDENCE: _____

4. <u>Persons Entitled to Citation</u>.

The mother of the child(ren) is _____, who is over 21 years of age and who resides at _____.

Process should be served at that address.

The father of the child(ren) is _____, who is over 21 years of age and who resides at _____.

Process should be served at that address.

There are no court-ordered conservatorships, court-ordered guardianships, or other court-ordered relationship affecting the children the subject of this suit.

5. <u>Property</u>.

No property is owned or possessed by the children the subject of this suit.

6. <u>Conservatorship</u>.

The parents of the children are or will be separated. It is in the best interest of the children that the Petitioner be appointed sole managing conservator of the children.

7. <u>Support</u>.

_____, Respondents, are obligated to support the children and should be ordered by the Court to make payments for the support of the children in the manner specified by the Court.

8. <u>Prayer</u>.

Petitioner prays that citation and notice issue as required by law and that the Court enter its orders in accordance with the foregoing allegations.

Petitioner prays for attorney's fees, expenses, and costs.

Petitioner prays for general relief.

Respectfully submitted,

BY:_____

Name:_____

BY:_____

Name:_____

Address:_____

_____

Telephone:_____

NO._____

IN THE INTEREST OF

*   IN THE DISTRICT COURT

*

*

*   _____ DISTRICT COURT

*

*

*

*

MINOR CHILDREN

*   _____ COUNTY, TEXAS

PETITION OF GRANDPARENT(S) FOR INTERVENTION
IN SUIT AFFECTING THE PARENT-CHILD RELATIONSHIP

1.   <u>Petitioner</u>.

This suit is brought by _____,
Petitioner(s), who is/are over 21 years of age and who reside(s) at_____
_____.

Petitioners are the grandmother and grandfather of the children the subject of this suit.

Petitioners have standing to bring this suit in that Petitioners would show the court that the child's present environment presents a serious and immediate question concerning the child's physical health or welfare.

2.   <u>Jurisdiction</u>.

No court has continuing jurisdiction of this suit or of the children the subject of this suit.

3.   <u>Children</u>.

The following children are the subject of this suit:

NAME: _____

SEX: _____

BIRTHPLACE: _____

BIRTH DATE: _____

PRESENT RESIDENCE: _____

NAME: _____

SEX: _____

BIRTHPLACE: _____

BIRTH DATE: _____

PRESENT RESIDENCE: _____

4.   <u>Persons Entitled to Citation.</u>
  The mother of the child(ren) is _____, who is over 21 years of age and who resides at _____.
  Process should be served at that address.
  The father of the child(ren) is _____, who is over 21 years of age and who resides at _____.
  Process should be served at that address.

5.   <u>Property.</u>
  No property is owned or possessed by the children the subject of this suit.

6.   <u>Conservatorship.</u>
  The parents of the children are or will be separated. It is in the best interest of the children that the Petitioner be appointed sole managing conservator of the children.

7.   <u>Support.</u>
  _____, Respondents, are obligated to support the children and should be ordered by the Court to make payments for the support of the children in the manner specified by the Court.

8.   <u>Prayer.</u>
  Petitioner prays that citation and notice issue as required by law and that the Court enter its orders in accordance with the foregoing allegations.
  Petitioner prays for attorney's fees, expenses, and costs.
  Petitioner prays for general relief.

                    Respectfully submitted,

                    BY:_____
                    Name:_____

                    BY:_____
                    Name:_____
                    Address:_____
                    _____
                    Telephone No._____

This action for child custody was heard before the Court on _____.
All interested parties appearing were given the opportunity to be heard and to present evidence.
On the evidence presented, the Court makes the following findings and orders:

<u>Jurisdiction</u>

The Court, having examined the pleadings and heard the evidence and argument of the parties, finds that it has jurisdiction of this cause and of all the parties and that no other court has continuing, exclusive jurisdiction of this cause. All persons entitled to notice of this action and final hearing were properly given notice.

<u>Custody</u>

IT IS ORDERED that _____

_____ shall have physical custody of the following children:

Visitation

IT IS ORDERED that _____

_____ shall have visitation with the children as follows:

Child Support

IT IS ORDERED that _____

shall pay child support in the amount of $_____ per _____, to

_____.

Costs

Costs of court are to be borne by _____.

Other Provisions

ORDERED on _____, _____.

_____

Judge

NO. _____

| In the Interest of | * | In the District Court |

_____, * _____ JUDICIAL DISTRICT

A CHILD * _____ COUNTY, TEXAS

DECREE FOR CHILD CUSTODY

On _____, hearing was held in this cause.

Appearances

Petitioners, _____appeared in person.

Respondents, _____appeared in person.

Jurisdiction

The Court, having examined the pleadings and heard the evidence and argument of the parties, finds that it has jurisdiction of this cause and of all the parties and that no other court has continuing, exclusive jurisdiction of this cause.

Findings

A jury was waived, and all questions of fact and of law were submitted to the Court. All persons entitled to citation were properly cited. The making of a record of testimony was:

waived by the parties with the consent of the Court

duly reported by_____.

The Court finds that the following children are the subject of this suit:

NAME: _____
SEX: _____
BIRTHPLACE: _____
BIRTH DATE: _____
HOME STATE: _____
SOCIAL SECURITY NO: _____
DRIVER'S LICENSE NO: _____

NAME: _____
SEX: _____
BIRTHPLACE: _____
BIRTH DATE: _____
HOME STATE: _____
SOCIAL SECURITY NO: _____
DRIVER'S LICENSE NO: _____

Conservatorship

The Court finds the following orders are in the best interest of the children:

IT IS ORDERED AND DECREED that _____ shall have physical custody of the following children: _____ _____.

Possession Order

IT IS ORDERED AND DECREED that _____ shall have access to the children as follows: _____ _____ _____ _____.

Costs

Costs of court are to be borne by _____.

Relief Not Granted

IT IS ORDERED AND DECREED that all relief requested in this cause and not expressly granted is denied.

Date of Judgment

SIGNED on _____, _____.

_____
JUDGE PRESIDING

MOTION FOR SOCIAL STUDY/ORDER

The undersigned, hereby move(s) this Court to order that a social study be conducted into the circumstances and condition of the child(ren) and of the homes of all parties seeking custody of, or visitation with, the child(ren) to determine the best interest of the child(ren) regarding custody and visitation.

Dated:_____

Signature _____
Name_____
Address_____

Telephone No._____

ORDER FOR SOCIAL STUDY

IN CONSIDERATION of the foregoing Motion for Social Study, and the Court being fully advised in the premises;

IT IS HEREBY ORDERED that _____

_____ shall conduct a social study into the circumstances and conditions of the child(ren) and of the homes of all persons seeking custody of, or visitation with, said child(ren), and shall file written findings and conclusions of the social study with the Court on or before _____.

ORDERED on _____.

_____
Judge

MOTION FOR APPOINTMENT OF GUARDIAN AD LITEM

The undersigned movant requests this court appoint a guardian ad litem and states:

1. This matter is before the Court on the undersigned movant's complaint / petition for custody of / visitation with the following minor child(ren):

Child(ren)
Name(s)   Date Of Birth   Age   Sex   Presently residing with

2. A guardian ad litem is necessary to protect the best interests of the child(ren).

3. Other court-ordered social investigations are:
   ___Home study
   ___Other (specify)_____

4. Payment of attorney's fees for guardian ad litem, at the reasonable rate of $_____/hr. shall be
   ___waived [indigence affidavit(s) filed].
   ___paid by _____.
   ___determined and allocated by court at conclusion of case.

5. The issues in this case require immediate action. It is requested that the guardian ad litem promptly complete the investigation and file the report with the court and serve copies on parties or counsel by _____.
                                     (date)

DATED: _____   _____

                                           Signature

                                           Name_____
                                           Address_____
                                           _____
                                           Telephone No._____

ORDER APPOINTING GUARDIAN AD LITEM

IN CONSIDERATION of the Motion to Appoint Guardian Ad Litem, and the Court being fully advised in the premises; the Court finds that it is in the best interests of the minor child(ren) in this case, that a guardian ad litem be appointed. Therefore, it is

ORDERED that

1. _____

(Name, address, telephone number)

_____

is hereby appointed guardian ad litem for the minor child(ren) in this matter. Counsel for the parties, or pro se parties should contact the guardian ad litem immediately.

2. <u>Authority of guardian ad litem</u>. Upon presentation of this order to any agency, hospital, organization, school, person, or office, public and private health facilities, medical and mental health professionals, including doctors, nurses, pediatricians, psychologists, psychiatrists, counselors and staff, and law enforcement agencies, the individual designated by this order is hereby authorized to inspect and copy any records relating to the child(ren), without the consent of the child(ren) or the parents of the child(ren).

3. <u>Confidentiality</u>. The guardian ad litem shall maintain any information received from any such source as confidential, and will not disclose the same except in reports to the court and other parties to this cause.

4.   Attendance at all proceedings. The guardian ad litem shall attend all depositions, hearings, and all proceedings scheduled in this case and shall assure proper representation of the child(ren)'s best interests at such proceedings.

5.   Notification. The guardian ad litem shall be notified of any depositions, hearings, investigations, or other proceedings, and shall be notified prior to any action which may affect the child(ren).

6.   Duties of guardian ad litem. The guardian ad litem, in addition to attendance at all proceedings, shall meet with the parties, their counsel, and the child(ren); may contact psychologists/counselors, family members, friends, neighbors, or school personnel, and shall conduct such other investigation as would assist the court in its determination of the best interests of the child(ren).

7.   Consultation prior to agreement. The guardian ad litem shall be consulted prior to any agreement or plan being entered into which affects the welfare of the child(ren).

8.   Report. The guardian ad litem shall file and serve upon counsel or pro se parties a report of court appointed guardian ad litem at least 1 week prior to the final hearing in this matter.

9.   Payment for services of guardian ad litem. An affidavit of indigence __has __has not been filed. Therefore, the guardian ad litem

___shall serve pro bono

___shall not serve pro bono and shall be paid for fees and costs incurred.

The fees and costs shall be

___ paid by _____

___determined at conclusion of case.

DATED:_____   _____

                                     JUDGE

Attorney for Petitioner or Petitioner   Attorney for Respondent or Respondent
Name_____   Name_____
Address_____   Address_____
_____   _____
Telephone No._____   Telephone No._____

Guardian ad Litem
Name_____
Address_____
_____
Telephone No._____

MOTION FOR PSYCHIATRIC / PSYCHOLOGICAL EXAMINATION

The movant(s), _____, respectfully request(s) that the court order psychiatric or psychological evaluation of the parties and minor child(ren) in this case, and states:

____ 1. The psychological condition of the party(ies) is at issue in this case and good cause therefore exists for psychological evaluation of:

      ____ Mother   ____ Father   ____ Child(ren)   ____ Movant(s)

      ____ Other (specify):_____

____ 2. <u>Payment for psychological evaluations.</u>

      ____Movant(s) is/are unable to pay and an affidavit of indigence in this case ___has ___has not been filed.

      ____Father ____Mother of the child(ren) is/are gainfully employed and well able to pay the costs of such evaluations.

      ____Father ____Mother ____Movant(s) are well able to contribute to the costs of evaluation, and movant(s) request the court order costs of evaluations be equitably divided between them.

DATED:_____

_____
Signature

I HEREBY CERTIFY THAT I have
___mailed
___hand delivered a
copy of this Motion on
_____ to:
Attorney for Opposing Party or Party
Name_____
Address_____

_____
Telefax No._____

Attorney for Moving Party or Party
Name_____
Address_____

_____
Telephone No._____

ORDER FOR PSYCHIATRIC / PSYCHOLOGICAL EXAMINATION

THE COURT having considered the motion for psychological evaluation, it is hereby:

ORDERED AND ADJUDGED that:

1.   The following psychologist/psychiatrist shall conduct a psychological evaluation of the parties and the children as soon as is expediently possible:

        Name_____

        Address_____

        Telephone No._____

2.   The evaluation shall concentrate on the following issues:

   ____   Custody   ____   Visitation and contact

   ____   Abuse/neglect allegations   ____   Other (specify):_____

3.   The parties or their counsel shall immediately contact the court-appointed psychologist/psychiatrist to assure scheduling for their clients and the minor child(ren).

4.   The original report shall be filed with the court, and a copy furnished to each pro se party or the attorney for each represented party.

5.   The court determines payment for such psychological evaluation as follows:

_____

_____

_____

_____

     The cost for each evaluation should not exceed $_____.

DATED:_____   _____
                                                JUDGE

Copies furnished to:
All counsel of record or pro se parties
Psychologist/psychiatrist

MOTION TO PROCEED IN FORMA PAUPERIS

The undersigned _____, hereby moves this Court to waive court filing fees and other costs associated with bringing this action, and allow the undersigned to proceed *in forma pauperis.* This motion is based upon the following facts and circumstances:

I am insolvent and unable to pay the charges, costs or fees otherwise payable by law to any clerk, or sheriff in this civil action because (choose one):

_____ a.   I am currently receiving public assistance: $_____
          per _____ Case No._____.

_____ b.   I am unable to pay those clerk's fees and costs because of indigence, based on the following facts:

INCOME: _____

_____
Employer name and address

_____
Length of employment

$_____ $_____
Avg. gross pay   Avg. net pay

per ____week ____month ____2 weeks

ASSETS: (State value of car, home, bank deposits, bonds, stocks, etc.)

OBLIGATIONS: (Itemize monthly rent, installment payments, mortgage payments, child support, etc.)

_____

Signature

Name_____

Address_____

_____

Telephone No._____

Acknowledged before me on _____, by _____
_____, who is personally known to me or produced
_____ as identification, and who did take an oath.

_____
NOTARY PUBLIC
My Commission Expires:

FINANCIAL AFFIDAVIT

STATE OF   )
COUNTY OF   )

      BEFORE ME, this day personally appeared _____,
who being duly sworn, deposes and says that the following information is true and correct:

EMPLOYMENT AND INCOME

OCCUPATION: _____
EMPLOYED BY: _____
ADDRESS: _____
                              _____

SOC. SEC. #:   _____
PAY PERIOD: _____
RATE OF PAY: _____

AVERAGE GROSS MONTHLY INCOME FROM EMPLOYMENT $_____

Bonuses, commissions, allowances, overtime, tips and similar payments   _____

Business Income from sources such as self-employment, partnership,
     close corporations, and/or independent contracts (gross receipts
     minus ordinary and necessary expenses required to produce income)   _____

Disability benefits   _____

Workers' Compensation   _____

Unemployment Compensation   _____

Pension, retirement, or annuity payments   _____

Social Security benefits   _____

Spousal support received from previous marriage   _____

Interest and dividends   _____

Rental income (gross receipts minus ordinary and necessary expenses
     required to produce income)   _____

Income from royalties, trusts, or estates   _____

Reimbursed expenses and in kind payments to the extent that they
    reduce personal living expenses   _____

Gains derived from dealing in property (not including nonrecurring gains)   _____

Itemize any other income of a recurring nature   _____

TOTAL MONTHLY INCOME $_____

LESS DEDUCTIONS:

Federal, state, and local income taxes (corrected for filing
    status and actual number of withholding allowances) $_____

FICA or self-employment tax (annualized)   _____

Mandatory union dues   _____

Mandatory retirement   _____

Health insurance payments   _____

Court ordered support payments for the children actually paid   _____

TOTAL DEDUCTIONS $_____

AVERAGE MONTHLY EXPENSES

HOUSEHOLD:

Mtg. or rent payments _____
Property taxes & insurance _____
Electricity _____
Water, garbage, & sewer _____
Telephone _____
Fuel oil or natural gas _____
Repairs and maintenance _____
Lawn and pool care _____
Pest control _____
Misc. household _____
Food and grocery items _____
Meals outside home _____
Other:

_____ _____
_____ _____

AUTOMOBILE:

Gasoline and oil _____
Repairs _____
Auto tags and license _____
Insurance _____
Other:

_____ _____
_____ _____

CHILDREN'S EXPENSES:

Nursery or babysitting _____
School tuition _____
School supplies _____
Lunch money _____
Allowance _____
Clothing _____
Medical, dental, prescriptions _____
Vitamins _____
Barber/beauty parlor _____

Cosmetics/toiletries _____
Gifts for special holidays _____
Other expenses:

_____ _____
_____ _____

CHILDREN'S EXPENSES:

Subtotal $_____

INSURANCES:

Health _____
Life _____
Other Insurance:

_____ _____

OTHER EXPENSES NOT LISTED ABOVE:

Dry cleaning and laundry _____
Affiant's clothing _____
Affiant's medical, dental, prescriptions _____
Affiant's beauty salon/barber _____
Affiant's gifts (special holidays) _____
Pets:
  Grooming _____
  Veterinarian _____
Membership Dues:
  Professional dues _____
  Social dues _____
Entertainment _____
Vacations _____
Publications _____
Religious organizations _____
Charities _____
Miscellaneous _____

OTHER EXPENSES:

_____   _____
_____   _____
_____   _____
_____   _____
_____   _____
_____   _____
_____   _____
_____   _____
_____   _____   TOTAL ABOVE EXPENSES $_____

PAYMENTS TO CREDITORS:

TO WHOM: BALANCE DUE: MONTHLY PAYMENTS:
_____   _____   _____
_____   _____   _____
_____   _____   _____
_____   _____   _____
_____   _____   _____
_____   _____   _____
_____   _____   _____
_____   _____   _____
_____   _____   _____

TOTAL MONTHLY PAYMENTS TO CREDITORS: $_____

TOTAL MONTHLY EXPENSES: $_____

ASSETS (OWNERSHIP: IF JOINT, ALLOCATE EQUITY)

Description	Value	Husband	Wife
Cash (on hand or in banks)	_____	_____	_____
Stocks/bonds/notes	_____	_____	_____
Real estate:			
Home:	_____	_____	_____
_____	_____	_____	_____
_____	_____	_____	_____
_____	_____	_____	_____
Automobiles:			
_____	_____	_____	_____
_____	_____	_____	_____
Other personal property:			
Contents of home	_____	_____	_____
Jewelry	_____	_____	_____
Life Ins./cash surrender value	_____	_____	_____
Other Assets:			
_____	_____	_____	_____
_____	_____	_____	_____
TOTAL ASSETS:	$_____	$_____	$_____

LIABILITIES

Creditor	Security	Balance	Husband	Wife
_____	_____	_____	_____	_____
_____	_____	_____	_____	_____
_____	_____	_____	_____	_____
_____	_____	_____	_____	_____
_____	_____	_____	_____	_____
_____	_____	_____	_____	_____
_____	_____	_____	_____	_____
_____	_____	_____	_____	_____
_____	_____	_____	_____	_____

TOTAL LIABILITIES: $_____ $_____ $_____

_____
Affiant's Signature

Acknowledged before me on _____, by _____
_____, who is personally known to me or produced _____ as
identification, and who did take an oath.

_____
NOTARY PUBLIC
My Commission Expires:

CERTIFICATE OF SERVICE

I HEREBY CERTIFY that a true and correct copy of the above was delivered by mail this
_____ day of _____, _____, to: _____.

_____
Signature
Name_____
Address_____
_____
Telephone No._____

AGREEMENT REGARDING

_____

The undersigned parties stipulate and agree to the following terms and conditions as full settlement of this action, and further agree that this agreement shall be incorporated into a final order:

This court shall retain jurisdiction to enforce the terms of this agreement.

DATED:_____   DATED:_____

_____   _____
Signature   Signature
Name:_____   Name:_____

_____   _____
Signature   Signature
Name:_____   Name:_____
Address:_____   Address:_____

_____   _____
Telephone No._____   Telephone No._____

MOTION TO SET HEARING

The _____ hereby moves the Court to set a hearing on the

matter of_____.

DATED:_____   _____

Signature

Name:_____

Address:_____

_____

Telephone:_____

ORDER

A hearing before the Court is set for _____, _____, at

_____ _____. m., at the following location:_____

_____.

_____

Judge

CERTIFICATE OF LAST KNOWN ADDRESS

Pursuant to rule _____ of the _____, I certify that the last known mailing address of the _____, _____, is

_____.

DATED:_____

_____

Signature

Name:_____

Address:_____

_____

Telephone No._____

INDEX

W

Your #1 Source for Real World Legal Information...

SPHINX® PUBLISHING
A Division of Sourcebooks, Inc.®
- Written by lawyers
- Simple English explanation of the law
- Forms and instructions included

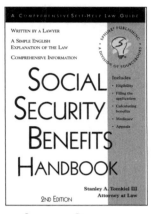

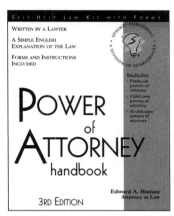

SOCIAL SECURITY BENEFITS HANDBOOK

Everything you need to know about social security benefits can be found in this book written by an attorney and former SSA representative.

212 pages; $14.95;
ISBN 1-57071-337-5

POWER OF ATTORNEY HANDBOOK, 3RD ED.

Forms and instructions are included to enable you to allow someone to act on your behalf for your convenience or necessity. Covers financial, health care, child care and real estate powers of attorney.

140 pages; $19.95;
ISBN 1-57071-348-0

HOW TO MAKE YOUR OWN WILL

Valid in 50 states, this book contains 14 different legal forms that will help consumers put their financial affairs in order. Also discusses inheritance laws.

144 pages; $12.95;
ISBN 1-57071-228-X

See the following order form for books written specifically for California, Florida, Georgia, Illinois, Massachusetts, Michigan, Minnesota, New York, North Carolina, Pennsylvania, and Texas! *Coming soon—Ohio and New Jersey!*

What our customers say about our books:

"It couldn't be more clear for the lay person." —R.D.

"I want you to know I really appreciate your book. It has saved me a lot of time and money." —L.T.

"Your real estate contracts book has saved me nearly $12,000.00 in closing costs over the past year." —A.B.

"...many of the legal questions that I have had over the years were answered clearly and concisely through your plain English interpretation of the law." —C.E.H.

"If there weren't people out there like you I'd be lost. You have the best books of this type out there." —S.B.

"...your forms and directions are easy to follow." —C.V.M.

Sphinx Publishing's Legal Survival Guides
are directly available from the Sourcebooks, Inc., or from your local bookstores.
For credit card orders call 1–800–43–BRIGHT, write P.O. Box 372, Naperville, IL 60566,
or fax 630-961-2168

SPHINX® PUBLISHING'S NATIONAL TITLES
Valid in All 50 States

LEGAL SURVIVAL IN BUSINESS

How to Form a Limited Liability Company (April)	$19.95
How to Form Your Own Corporation (2E)	$19.95
How to Form Your Own Partnership	$19.95
How to Register Your Own Copyright (2E)	$19.95
How to Register Your Own Trademark (2E)	$19.95
Most Valuable Business Legal Forms You'll Ever Need (2E)	$19.95
Most Valuable Corporate Forms You'll Ever Need (2E)	$24.95
Software Law (with diskette)	$29.95

LEGAL SURVIVAL IN COURT

Crime Victim's Guide to Justice	$19.95
Debtors' Rights (3E)	$12.95
Defend Yourself against Criminal Charges	$19.95
Grandparents' Rights (2E)	$19.95
Help Your Lawyer Win Your Case	$12.95
Jurors' Rights (2E)	$9.95
Legal Malpractice and Other Claims against Your Lawyer (2E) (June)	$18.95
Legal Research Made Easy (2E)	$14.95
Simple Ways to Protect Yourself from Lawsuits	$24.95
Victims' Rights	$12.95
Winning Your Personal Injury Claim	$19.95

LEGAL SURVIVAL IN REAL ESTATE

How to Buy a Condominium or Townhome	$16.95
How to Negotiate Real Estate Contracts (3E)	$16.95
How to Negotiate Real Estate Leases (3E)	$16.95
Successful Real Estate Brokerage Management	$19.95

LEGAL SURVIVAL IN PERSONAL AFFAIRS

How to File Your Own Bankruptcy (4E)	$19.95
How to File Your Own Divorce (3E)	$19.95
How to Make Your Own Will	$12.95
How to Write Your Own Living Will	$9.95
How to Write Your Own Premarital Agreement (2E)	$19.95
How to Win Your Unemployment Compensation Claim	$19.95
Living Trusts and Simple Ways to Avoid Probate (2E)	$19.95
Neighbors' Rights	$12.95
The Power of Attorney Handbook (3E)	$19.95
Simple Ways to Protect Yourself from Lawsuits	$24.95
Social Security Benefits Handbook (2E)	$14.95
Unmarried Parents' Rights	$19.95
U.S.A. Immigration Guide (3E)	$19.95
Guia de Inmigracion a Estados Unidos (2E) (May)	$19.95

Legal Survival Guides are directly available from Sourcebooks, Inc., or from your local bookstores.

For credit card orders call 1–800–43–BRIGHT, write P.O. Box 372, Naperville, IL 60566,
or fax 630-961-2168

SPHINX® PUBLISHING ORDER FORM

BILL TO:		SHIP TO:	
Phone #	Terms	F.O.B. Chicago, IL	Ship Date

Charge my: ☐ VISA ☐ MasterCard ☐ American Express

☐ **Money Order or Personal Check**

Credit Card Number

Expiration Date

Qty	ISBN	Title	Retail	Ext.
		SPHINX PUBLISHING NATIONAL TITLES		
_____	1-57071-166-6	Crime Victim's Guide to Justice	$19.95	_____
_____	1-57071-342-1	Debtors' Rights (3E)	$12.95	_____
_____	1-57071-162-3	Defend Yourself against Criminal Charges	$19.95	_____
_____	1-57248-082-3	Grandparents' Rights (2E)	$19.95	_____
_____	1-57248-087-4	Guia de Inmigracion a Estados Unidos (2E) (May)	$19.95	_____
_____	1-57248-021-1	Help Your Lawyer Win Your Case	$12.95	_____
_____	1-57071-164-X	How to Buy a Condominium or Townhome	$16.95	_____
_____	1-57071-223-9	How to File Your Own Bankruptcy (4E)	$19.95	_____
_____	1-57071-224-7	How to File Your Own Divorce (3E)	$19.95	_____
_____	1-57248-083-1	How to Form a Limited Liability Company (April)	$19.95	_____
_____	1-57071-227-1	How to Form Your Own Corporation (2E)	$19.95	_____
_____	1-57071-343-X	How to Form Your Own Partnership	$19.95	_____
_____	1-57071-228-X	How to Make Your Own Will	$12.95	_____
_____	1-57071-331-6	How to Negotiate Real Estate Contracts (3E)	$16.95	_____
_____	1-57071-332-4	How to Negotiate Real Estate Leases (3E)	$16.95	_____
_____	1-57071-225-5	How to Register Your Own Copyright (2E)	$19.95	_____
_____	1-57071-226-3	How to Register Your Own Trademark (2E)	$19.95	_____
_____	1-57071-349-9	How to Win Your Unemployment Compensation Claim	$19.95	_____
_____	1-57071-167-4	How to Write Your Own Living Will	$9.95	_____
_____	1-57071-344-8	How to Write Your Own Premarital Agreement (2E)	$19.95	_____
_____	1-57071-333-2	Jurors' Rights (2E)	$9.95	_____
_____	1-57248-090-4	Legal Malpractice and Other Claims against...(2E) (June)	$18.95	_____
_____	1-57071-400-2	Legal Research Made Easy (2E)	$14.95	_____
_____	1-57071-336-7	Living Trusts and Simple Ways to Avoid Probate (2E)	$19.95	_____
_____	1-57071-345-6	Most Valuable Bus. Legal Forms You'll Ever Need (2E)	$19.95	_____
_____	1-57071-346-4	Most Valuable Corporate Forms You'll Ever Need (2E)	$24.95	_____

Qty	ISBN	Title	Retail	Ext.
_____	1-57248-089-0	Neighbors' Rights	$12.95	_____
_____	1-57071-348-0	The Power of Attorney Handbook (3E)	$19.95	_____
_____	1-57248-020-3	Simple Ways to Protect Yourself from Lawsuits	$24.95	_____
_____	1-57071-337-5	Social Security Benefits Handbook (2E)	$14.95	_____
_____	1-57071-163-1	Software Law (w/diskette)	$29.95	_____
_____	0-913825-86-7	Successful Real Estate Brokerage Mgmt.	$19.95	_____
_____	1-57071-399-5	Unmarried Parents' Rights	$19.95	_____
_____	1-57071-354-5	U.S.A. Immigration Guide (3E)	$19.95	_____
_____	0-913825-82-4	Victims' Rights	$12.95	_____
_____	1-57071-165-8	Winning Your Personal Injury Claim	$19.95	_____
		CALIFORNIA TITLES		
_____	1-57071-360-X	CA Power of Attorney Handbook	$12.95	_____
_____	1-57071-355-3	How to File for Divorce in CA	$19.95	_____
_____	1-57071-356-1	How to Make a CA Will	$12.95	_____
_____	1-57071-408-8	How to Probate an Estate in CA (April)	$19.95	_____
_____	1-57071-357-X	How to Start a Business in CA	$16.95	_____
_____	1-57071-358-8	How to Win in Small Claims Court in CA	$14.95	_____
_____	1-57071-359-6	Landlords' Rights and Duties in CA	$19.95	_____
		FLORIDA TITLES		
_____	1-57071-363-4	Florida Power of Attorney Handbook (2E)	$12.95	_____
_____	1-57248-093-9	How to File for Divorce in FL (6E) (July)	$21.95	_____
_____	1-57248-086-6	How to Form a Limited Liability Co. in FL (April)	$19.95	_____
_____	1-57071-401-0	How to Form a Partnership in FL	$19.95	_____
_____	1-57071-380-4	How to Form a Corporation in FL (4E)	$19.95	_____
_____	1-57071-361-8	How to Make a FL Will (5E)	$12.95	_____
_____	1-57248-088-2	How to Modify Your FL Divorce Judgement (4E) (May)	$22.95	_____

Form Continued on Following Page   **SUBTOTAL** _____

SPHINX® PUBLISHING ORDER FORM

Qty	ISBN	Title	Retail	Ext.
		FLORIDA TITLES (CONT'D)		
	1-57071-364-2	How to Probate an Estate in FL (3E)	$24.95	
	1-57248-081-5	How to Start a Business in FL (5E) (March)	$16.95	
	1-57071-362-6	How to Win in Small Claims Court in FL (6E)	$14.95	
	1-57071-335-9	Landlords' Rights and Duties in FL (7E)	$19.95	
	1-57071-334-0	Land Trusts in FL (5E)	$24.95	
	0-913825-73-5	Women's Legal Rights in FL	$19.95	
		GEORGIA TITLES		
	1-57071-376-6	How to File for Divorce in GA (3E)	$19.95	
	1-57248-075-0	How to Make a GA Will (3E)	$12.95	
	1-57248-076-9	How to Start a Business in Georgia (3E)	$16.95	
		ILLINOIS TITLES		
	1-57071-405-3	How to File for Divorce in IL (2E)	$19.95	
	1-57071-415-0	How to Make an IL Will (2E)	$12.95	
	1-57071-416-9	How to Start a Business in IL (2E)	$16.95	
	1-57248-078-5	Landlords' Rights & Duties in IL (February)	$19.95	
		MASSACHUSETTS TITLES		
	1-57071-329-4	How to File for Divorce in MA (2E)	$19.95	
	1-57248-050-5	How to Make a MA Will	$9.95	
	1-57248-053-X	How to Probate an Estate in MA	$19.95	
	1-57248-054-8	How to Start a Business in MA	$16.95	
	1-57248-055-6	Landlords' Rights and Duties in MA	$19.95	
		MICHIGAN TITLES		
	1-57071-409-6	How to File for Divorce in MI (2E)	$19.95	
	1-57248-077-7	How to Make a MI Will (2E)	$12.95	
	1-57071-407-X	How to Start a Business in MI (2E)	$16.95	
		MINNESOTA TITLES		
	1-57248-039-4	How to File for Divorce in MN	$19.95	
	1-57248-040-8	How to Form a Simple Corporation in MN	$19.95	
	1-57248-037-8	How to Make a MN Will	$9.95	
	1-57248-038-6	How to Start a Business in MN	$16.95	
		NEW YORK TITLES		
	1-57071-184-4	How to File for Divorce in NY (March)	$19.95	
	1-57248-095-5	How to Make a NY Will (2E)	$12.95	
	1-57071-185-2	How to Start a Business in NY	$16.95	
	1-57071-187-9	How to Win in Small Claims Court in NY	$14.95	
	1-57071-186-0	Landlords' Rights and Duties in NY (March)	$19.95	
	1-57071-188-7	New York Power of Attorney Handbook	$19.95	
		NORTH CAROLINA TITLES		
	1-57071-326-X	How to File for Divorce in NC (2E)	$19.95	
	1-57071-327-8	How to Make a NC Will (2E)	$12.95	
	1-57248-096-3	How to Start a Business in NC (2E)	$16.95	
	1-57248-091-2	Landlords' Rights & Duties in NC (June)	$19.95	
		PENNSYLVANIA TITLES		
	1-57071-177-1	How to File for Divorce in PA	$19.95	
	1-57248-094-7	How to Make a PA Will (2E)	$12.95	
	1-57071-178-X	How to Start a Business in PA	$16.95	
	1-57071-179-8	Landlords' Rights and Duties in PA (June)	$19.95	
		TEXAS TITLES		
	1-57071-330-8	How to File for Divorce in TX (2E)	$19.95	
	1-57248-009-2	How to Form a Simple Corporation in TX	$19.95	
	1-57071-417-7	How to Make a TX Will (2E)	$12.95	
	1-57071-418-5	How to Probate an Estate in TX (2E)	$19.95	
	1-57071-365-0	How to Start a Business in TX (2E)	$16.95	
	1-57248-012-2	How to Win in Small Claims Court in TX	$14.95	
	1-57248-011-4	Landlords' Rights and Duties in TX	$19.95	

SUBTOTAL THIS PAGE _____

SUBTOTAL PREVIOUS PAGE _____

Illinois residents add 6.75% sales tax
Florida residents add 6% state sales tax plus applicable discretionary surtax _____

Shipping— $4.00 for 1st book, $1.00 each additional _____

TOTAL _____